A WALKING GUIDE TO

NEW ZEALAND'S LONG TRAIL

Te ARAROA

A WALKING GUIDE TO NEW ZEALAND'S LONG TRAIL

Te ARAROA

— GEOFF CHAPPLE —

RANDOM HOUSE
NEW ZEALAND

To those who love the New Zealand outdoors

RANDOM HOUSE

UK | USA | Canada | Ireland | Australia
India | New Zealand | South Africa | China

Random House is an imprint of the Penguin Random House group of companies, whose addresses can be found at global.penguinrandomhouse.com.

Penguin
Random House
New Zealand

A catalogue record for this book is available from the National Library of New Zealand

First published 2011. Reprinted 2012, 2015, 2016, 2019. Reprinted and updated 2013, 2014, 2017.

© 2011 text Te Araroa Trust; photographs remains with individual copyright holders as credited on page 276; C.K. Stead's 'The Shore' on page 70 and The Topp Twins' 'Turangawaewae' on page 82 are used with kind permission.

The moral rights of the author have been asserted

ISBN 978 1 86979 714 0

Design: Nick Turzynski, redinc, Auckland
Front cover photograph: Amos Chapple
Back cover photographs: Amos Chapple, Razzu Engen, Amos Chapple
Maps by Geographx
Prepress by Image Centre Group
Printed and bound in China by RR Donnelley Asia Printing Solutions Ltd

For their contribution to the mapping costs for this book, Te Araroa Trust thanks:

WALKING**ACCESS**
ARA HĪKOI AOTEAROA

ASB Community Trust
Te Kaitiaki Putea o Tamaki o Tai Tokerau
supported by 'ASB

Department of
Conservation
Te Papa Atawhai

The Tindall
Foundation

Contents

Lake Tekapo from Stag Saddle.

Preface

THIS BOOK IS A GUIDE for those who may want simply to browse Te Araroa's single bright line as it runs, map by consecutive map, down the length of the country. It's also a guide for active walkers, who may use it to day-walk some of the tracks that together make up Te Araroa's 3000 km length. Finally, it's a guide for those who intend walking the entire length, the through-tramper in a sustained endeavour, or the section-tramper, ticking off over time the tracks that make up the whole route.

I'd also call the book a companion to Te Araroa itself. I've always regarded the trail as struggling to be born, and here it is. By way of its maps, its photographs and its text, this book gives the trail its voice.

Te Araroa has until lately been something of a mystery to most New Zealanders. Our resources were always slim, land negotiations were always slow, budgets were hard to put together and official support did not really swing in until quite late in the piece. Our main strength in the early years was that we did not give up. It started as a volunteer effort and remains a volunteer effort mainly, perhaps one of the greatest this country has known. There are people to thank.

Traver's River.

Gary Leigh installs signage, Onekainga Track.

Introduction

THE WORLD'S GREAT TRAILS — the Appalachian Trail, the Bruce Trail, the Pennine Way to name a few — are all trails along a single geographic feature. They may follow an escarpment or a mountain range, occasionally a coast, and sometimes even a man-made feature like the remnants of Hadrian's Wall, but whatever it is, long trails seem to have that unity.

Te Araroa — translated as The Long Pathway — would hope to sidle into such illustrious company. It would claim its unity is more than the sunlit surface of its geography. Something unlit. Below New Zealand lie two opposing lithospheric plates, and if you walk this country, you walk a land that has been, on the back of those underlying plates, thoroughly tugged about. The trail's unity is that singular force. Every basin and range, every mountain and plain, every thermal pool and volcanic hump exists because of it. The trail's unity is its variety, and even before setting foot on whatever part of its length you choose, it seems proper to consider briefly how that variety came about. Brief is good, and if every million years that has passed since this country's separation from Gondwana is shrunk to a second, the clip need take only 80 seconds.

When the separation takes place, the land that rafts away from Gondwana is continental in size and, like any continent of the time, it carries a hooting cargo of dinosaurs. They'll roam for 15 seconds across a land mass half the size of Australia.

Then they're gone. The Chicxulub asteroid impact on the other side of the globe ruined their world — or so we think.

Then the continent, with whatever remnant species had survived that cataclysm, slowly drowns. No one knows quite how long that took, but they do know the waves closed over, perhaps completely, so that much of the clip may be nothing but that blue surface. The last 22 seconds, though, are worth watching.

The lithosphere sunders beneath the sunken continent. Two plates contend. One overrides the other or simply goes head to head and slides sideways. Volcanic chains rise out of the sea, and a sliver of the original undersea craton is uplifted around them. Rising fastest of all is the southern welt of the Alps. And that's it. Those volcanic ribs, the webbing between them, the great body of greywacke, the white skin of limestone . . . to be honest, the whole thing doesn't seem very different from Maui hauling up a huge fish. But however it's expressed, Aotearoa — the name by which this new land will report to the future — has arisen. Hundreds of years on from that first naming, a Dutch sea captain, Abel Tasman, will come by. He'll write in his log of 'a land uplifted high' and his discovery will yield another name — New Zealand.

A SHORT HISTORY OF LONG WALKING IN NEW ZEALAND

Maori traded and gifted down the entire length of Aotearoa — greenstone, volcanic glass, kumara, dried fish, nets, weaving. They went to war with mere, taiaha or musket, and some tracks were opened and maintained specifically as warpaths. They set up pou rahui — indicated by glyphs on the track which might reassure its walkers, or terrify them, and drew lizards in the caves. Maori runners wore flax sandals and travelled long distances.

It's worth noting that in the 1830s, at around the same time New Zealand's early Europeans were arriving, the ex-Napoleonic soldier Claude François Denecourt was secretly daubing trees and stones within a forest belonging to the French king. Blue paint pot to hand, Denecourt marked up trails that perhaps for the first time were entirely different from the trading or trekking trails of old. They would be public and walked for pleasure, passing deliberately by a grotto, or a waterfall, or a gnarled tree. The old soldier drew maps, published them, and the salon crowds of Paris flocked by train to Fontainebleau Forest, maps in hand, to experience a choice of trails, short, medium or long.

New Zealand's early Europeans walked, but were not French flâneurs. The disgraced missionary William Colenso walked, driven to discover and annotate a new botany. The mayor-to-be of Auckland, John Logan Campbell, walked north to the Bay of Islands, determined to expand his business. Bishop Augustus Selwyn walked, impelled by pastoral duty to cover 1500 km within six months of his arrival. Governor George Grey walked. In 1849, he journeyed with Iwikau Te Heu Heu, paramount chief of Tuwharetoa, from Auckland to Pukawa village on the southern shores of Lake Taupo for the tangi of Iwikau's brother, killed in a landslide. The journey, mostly overland and often through swampland and bush, took a month.

That early walking, along with everything that goes with it — the wide gaze across landscape, the self-reliance, the sense of the common earth — is still imprinted in New Zealand. Maori always had the wide gaze, but Pakeha too, recoiling from a loss of commons in their native England, Scotland and Ireland sought something of the same. Government surveyors marked out Maori land that passed through the Crown for sale with a 22 yard strip, the Queen's Chain, preserving public access along coastlines and waterways. The access was never perfectly achieved, but the Queen's Chain became emblematic of a right to fish in rivers and lakes, and use the coast unhindered.

In the 1880s, Donald Sutherland and Quinton McKinnon cut the Milford Track, and that considerable feat is a further milestone in this country's walking history. The trampers who followed noted the deep and distant views onto the old rock of Fiordland, the shake of avalanche, the red underside of kea wings above Mackinnon Pass, and the ropey battering dealt out by the Sutherland Falls. It was wilder and more remote than anything out of Fontainebleau, but the Milford Track was New Zealand's first public track without purpose beyond an encounter with the beautiful, the memorable, the sublime.

Track history moved up another notch as New Zealand's cities matured, along with the need of city crowds for recreation. The gaze of desk-bound Wellingtonians onto their snow-capped northern skyline inspired the first volunteer-led tracks. The Tararua Tramping Club developed the first tramping track and huts in the Tararua Range in the 1920s, and other local tramping clubs joined the effort. Together they established an extensive track system in the range, and the huts that would shelter their trampers.

el Sandford and Geoff Chapple bridging a stream, Pehitawa Track.

In the 1940s and 1950s a man goes walking who has in his haversack a spare suit, boot polish and brush, pyjamas, a small bottle of ink, a fountain pen, a pair of slippers, a pocket book of hymns and the New Testament. No history of long walking in New Zealand can be complete without him, but he stands at an eccentric angle to his time, for his expeditions are, in the main, the then unheard of front-country walks. They resemble English country walks except they're not. There are fences to get over rather than kissing gates to close, animal tracks to follow rather than winding paths, crumbling cliffs to climb rather than steps to ascend. The man is a publisher, and has an excellent nose for New Zealand's social history. He walks, observes accurately and publishes his journals, *Farthest East* (1945), *Farthest North* (1946), *Farthest West* (1950), and *Farthest South* (1952). He becomes New Zealand's gaunt old giant of walking, and his name is A.H. Reed. In 1960, at age 85, he walks on the roads from North Cape to Bluff, and people clap him through.

In the same period the New Zealand government was developing back-country tracks and huts for forestry and deer culling. Barry Crump's *A Good Keen Man* (1960) documents the era of deer hunters in the Ruahine, Kaweka and Urewera ranges. Aside from the Tourist Hotel Corporation's oversight of the Milford Track and walks at a few other tourist centres, government interest in recreational tracks was slight, but throughout New Zealand by then, following the Tararua example, do-it-yourself tramping clubs were building their own huts, or taking over government huts when the hunters and foresters moved on.

In 1967, Bob Ussher, then president of the Alpine Sports Club, suggested to his executive the idea of a scenic trail from Cape Reinga to Bluff. The Federated Mountain Clubs (FMC), umbrella group for New Zealand's tramping fraternity, supported the proposal, and a knowledgeable group sketched a possible trail route on a Mobil road map.

The proposal went first to the Minister of Lands, Duncan MacIntyre, made halting progress through Wellington's back rooms, and resulted finally in the New Zealand Walkways Act 1975. The act set up the New Zealand Walkways Commission, the first-ever government body with a specific warrant to create walkways.

Bob Ussher's simple 1967 proposal had led to a new government-funded Commission dedicated to developing tracks, also along the trail, which was listed as its No. 2 objective. Yet within its first year Brian Hunt, the commission's FMC representative, and the keeper, if any existed, of the FMC's vision of a long New Zealand trail, stated publicly, 'Initially the concept was for a series of connecting walkways from Cape Reinga to Bluff. However, it soon became apparent that it was more important to concentrate on shorter walkways adjacent to large centres of population with the idea that these shorter walks would ultimately become part of the overall trail network.'

In a 10 year run, the commission put in 130 walkways but was then disestablished. In 1989 the newly established Department of Conservation inherited not just the commission's walkways, but tracks from the Wildlife Service, the Forest Service, and the National Parks Division of the Department of Lands and Survey — a combined total of 11,000 km, many in bad condition, and many where the tramping corridor was not legally secure. DOC's budgets were low and its mandate was far wider than walkways. No surprise then that it chose not to increase, but to shrink the track system.

TE ARAROA — THE LONG PATHWAY — ARRIVES

In 1994 I wrote a newspaper story that invoked a long trail — a reincarnation of a path that had once existed and had been forgotten. This was unprovable but I believed it was true.

At that time, I knew nothing of New Zealand's long-trail history. As a journalist I'd been aware of the Walkways Commission but only in its last years as a moribund quango. The long-trail spark had come from a close friend, William Ball. We'd worked together on company computer fitouts, pulling cables in industrial ceilings, and from time to time we'd have lunch together and talk.

On one such lunch, months before, we'd talked long trails. Will liked wilderness, and self-sufficiency, and log cabins — why not a trail young people might build? — and if I were to characterise myself then I simply liked the idea of a New Zealand-long exploration with everything thrown in — a trail to show New Zealanders their own country. In 1976, two of my friends, Geoff Steven and Phil Dadson, had filmed and sound-recorded the Maori land march from Cape Reinga to Wellington. The poet Hone Tuwhare was on that march and something he said then stuck in my mind. 'To know Papatuanuku,' said Hone, 'you have to go through slowly, on foot.'

My own walks were usually off the beaten track — Farewell Spit, Ball Pass, the Mt Arthur Tableland, even the Auckland Harbour Bridge as a marathon runner. My wife, Miriam Beatson, a self-taught bush botanist, also loved getting out there. As a *Listener* journalist I'd travelled often through New Zealand, taken a house bus around much of it with Miriam and our three children, and had written two social-history books. All these things conspired, but if you wanted a cap for everything then it was the people. New Zealand culture is unique. It's blunt, practical, loyal, funny, idiosyncratic . . . If anything justifies our nationality and pride, this is probably it, and it's strongest outside the cities. Trail country.

Add in the fact of 9 per cent unemployment in the 1990s, and the feeling of a nation sundered by the market reforms of those years. The long trail burst from this opaque pool of causality, and it came out under deadline pressure, late at night, and red hot. I wrote it quickly and sat back. The trail didn't exist, but it was important to name it. The spare intelligence and title of a book I'd read in 1986 came back to me — *The Long Pathway: Te Ara Roa* by Denis McLean. The former Deputy High Commissioner in London, together with his wife, Anne, and three children, had returned to New Zealand and reoriented themselves by walking the long coast from the East Cape to Wellington.

Te Araroa. It was the name of the East Cape town where the McLean family had begun. Denis had named the town with respect, then had gone on to use the wider meaning. I did the same.

My journalist friends mocked it — 'the shining path' — or defrocked it — 'your notional trail' — but the popular response was immediate and enthusiastic. The mayor of the then Waitakere City, Bob Harvey, loved the idea and suggested a trust to pursue it further. I was keen. Government agencies had recoiled from the task, but the response to the story convinced me that the idea remained in the popular culture like one of those birthday candles that reignite after being firmly blown out.

My editor, Jenny Wheeler, and I got the trust together, and Bob became chair. We ran a newspaper campaign in its favour. In 1995, we put in our first linking track from Kerikeri to Waitangi, signing it through on forestry roads, and it was easy. Prime Minister Jim

Bolger opened it, and the event got front-page treatment in *The New Zealand Herald*. Te Araroa Trust's (TAT) deed of trust decreed that TAT's efforts to inspire track building in the Northland and Auckland area would provide a successful model for the rest of the country. We'd done the demo. We all had other jobs and it was DOC and regional and local councils that had the track-building skills, so why reinvent the wheel? We gave presentations. We beat the ground around such agencies, as was our defined role. Take it guys, this idea that New Zealand wants to realise, and run with it. Nothing happened.

We began to consider other long trails and their definitions. American trails legislation listed three categories of trail — scenic, historic, and recreational. Te Araroa had to be all three. It was scenic, but we'd take it past historic spots, too. In the American legislation, recreational meant peri-urban, and we'd do that, too — take it through the cities, and the small towns. A high proportion of it would become, by that decision, a front-country track as well as the traditional back-country routes.

The trail shaped up conceptually, but still none of the track-building agencies moved. Even if a council was prepared to take a trail through its jurisdiction, it had no way of knowing where the beginning and end points should be. In 1997 I threw a suitcase into my car, and visited 27 of the regional and local authorities in the North Island, six DOC conservancies, and some of the Maori tribes. I put to them our plans. I listened to their own plans. I produced TAT's first publication *Te Araroa — North Island Foot Trail*. It was primitive but it had maps, and showed a way through that had a broad consensus of support.

Later that same year and on into the summer of 1998 I walked the route to test it, and posted on the internet, with primitive digital pictures, one of this country's first blogs — a real-time description of the tramp. Te Araroa became if not yet a trail then at least a popular website. The dedicated individuals and groups who would set the trail in place began to emerge, and the first substantial grant came in that year. Still, none of the agencies was constructing trails on our behalf, so by default we turned from a ginger group into a track-building group. Noel Sandford, a great back-country carpenter, put his hand up as construction manager. He put together subsidised Taskforce Green teams, did the work on low budgets, and Sir Edmund Hillary opened the trails.

In 2002 I completed TAT's second publication *Te Araroa — South Island Trail*, walked it and posted another blog. Then, with support from the Mayors Taskforce for Jobs, we began to construct in the south too. What followed was epic. Tracks across a mountain top, tracks up rivers, tracks over farmland, tracks along old water races. We signed a memorandum of understanding with DOC that declared its support and laid down protocols for construction on the Public Conservation Lands (PCL), though we had still to fund those tracks. In 2004 we signed up the first of eight Te Araroa regional trusts. Their mission was to fine-tune the route through their regions, to negotiate access and to raise funds for construction. They often won the access permissions, the support from their councils, and the funding that would have been impossible for the Auckland-based TAT.

The necessary finance began to arrive. In 2006, the ASB Community Trust granted TAT $1.7 million to advance the trail in the Northland and Auckland areas. In 2007 Helen Clark's Labour government allocated $3.8 million to DOC to take the trail across the PCL. DOC gained also an ongoing annual maintenance budget of $875,000 for its section of Te Araroa — at a stroke, 45 per cent of the trail distance was off our hands. These events freed

ormal opening of the connecting track to Mangawhai Coastal Walkway.

TAT and the regional trusts to concentrate on what we do best — by our leadership and influence to persuade councils into the effort, and where necessary to negotiate private-land crossing and track construction ourselves.

Track construction began to really roll. TAT had never doubted it would complete the trail, but the difference now was that others outside the trust began to believe the same. In 2011 John Key's National government allocated TAT $1.5 million to help build the last major links.

Gaps still exist. Property negotiation can take years, and some of that negotiation is ongoing. Rather than have through-walkers wait those extra years, TAT has mapped road bypasses that connect to the next trailhead. These less-than-perfect sections won't overly concern the majority of Te Araroa's users, who may use local parts of the longer trail simply as stand-alone day- or multi-day walks.

The trail route will continually be improved in these and other ways and readers of this book should consult TAT's website www.teararoa.org.nz to get the most up-to-date information. With every passing month there'll be change, but the basic route is now in place, in perpetuity — time that reaches into the future, but which equally reaches back.

New Zealand's past explorers and scouts and traders crossed the forests on the most obvious connecting ridges and Te Araroa uses at least some of the same ones. Where the grain of the ridges stood against the direction of travel, those former walkers sought out the saddles and passes, and Te Araroa uses many of those, too. When the ridges above were dangerously high, the ancestral walkers used river valleys, and they used the sandy thoroughfare of the coast. As does Te Araroa.

In these ways the trail is old, and now it begins to be new again. It's 3000 km long, from Cape Reinga to Bluff. It's not perfect, but it's there, and it will only get better. It's yours, New Zealand. Use it as you will.

New hut en route, Red Hills Hut, Richmond Alpine Track.

Old hut en route, Crooked Spur Hut, Two Thumb Track.

Using this book

TE ARAROA IS A 3000 KM TRAIL that extends from Cape Reinga in the north to Bluff in the south. There can be occasional track closures due to access restrictions, track damage or maintenance, farming activities such as lambing, or because a logging harvest has made it unavailable for a year or more. The trail goes around such closures by road bypass — consult TAT's website www.teararoa.org.nz for details.

The trail is walkable by moderately fit trampers and walkers with basic skills, though some 10 per cent of the distance is classified as 'route', a formal description meaning advanced back-country skills are advisable. The route component will be reduced over time. TAT's goal is a trail that's tramping-track standard or better along its whole length.

The book is divided into a North Island and a South Island trail. The separate islands are then divided into regions, five in the north and four in the the south. The nine regions are distinctive, and the book provides an introduction to each.

The regional trail descriptions are divided into two categories:

Tracks These are integral to the Te Araroa trail's through route but can be used also as stand-alone tramps or walks. The sidebar alongside the track description summarises start point, end point, distance and grade for those who want to use them in this way.

Connectors These patch through, off-road where possible, the distances between tracks. The connectors will interest mainly through- and section walkers, though they may have good short walks embedded within their length. They have no sidebar. The descriptions are brief, and indicated by the use of italics. More details of the connectors, including exact distances, are available on TAT's website.

Te Araroa is still evolving and any book that describes it will date. Most of the tracks listed here will stay in place, but some routes are still being added. The text notes where these new routes are under way, and those intending to walk these sections should check TAT's website www.teararoa.org.nz which will have the latest status report.

Please note, the Geographx maps within this book are not suitable for any tramping that requires map navigation, for two reasons:
- They're 1:240,000 scale (trampers traditionally use 1:50,000).
- They're obliquely angled, which foreshortens distance.

The sidebars on each track list three track standards:

Easy tramping A well-graded track that offers comfortable walking.

Tramping A challenging day, or multi-day, walk requiring some experience and self-sufficiency en route.

Hard tramping The most challenging of Te Araroa's tracks, always multi-day and route standard only. These tracks demand advanced back-country skills.

The sidebar to each track description also includes one or more map numbers. Those numbers refer to 1:50,000 map sections downloadable from TAT's website. The downloadable maps have the NZTM grid superimposed, and sufficient topographical detail, at A3 size, to tramp by. If you use these downloaded maps in the field, make sure you waterproof them.

Te Araroa's 3000 km route from Cape Reinga in the north to Bluff in the south.

Any long trail poses physical and logistical challenges for its through-walkers. Te Araroa Trust has researched the trail route and trail corridor to collect supporting information on planning, equipment, food drops, resupply points, water and toilet stops, campgrounds, local internet cafés, post offices, park service offices, requisite fitness levels, seasonal hazards and many other tips. The information is too particular, and too subject to revision, to be included in this book, but is collected together in trail notes and other information, available from TAT's website. A trail community is beginning to emerge around Te Araroa and awareness and support is constantly growing.

VOCABULARY

The text uses certain abbreviations regularly. Te Araroa Trust, the overall body in charge of the trail route, together with its regional trusts, is TAT. The Department of Conservation, which has control of some 45 per cent of the trail distance, is DOC.

Maori and Pakeha words that occur without explanation in the main text are listed in the glossary on page 274. The glossary also defines geological terms and lists in greater detail the plants and animals referred to.

Tramping Te Araroa

DIRECTION

Through-trampers predominantly walk the trail from north to south. New Zealand's long descent through the latitudes from a sub-tropical north to a sub-Antarctic south determines this decision. The tramping season in the North Island is longer and more flexible, while tramping in the South Island should be more carefully programmed to take advantage of the south's most settled weather between January and April.

Fast trampers complete Te Araroa in 120 days, including a few rest days, or less. The more moderate take 160 tramping days or more, but the 120- to 160-day range accommodates most, and influences planning. Overseas trampers should know that tramping speed on the North Island's bush tracks doesn't average much over 2.5 km an hour.

From Cape Reinga, a good start time for a through-tramper is from mid-November to the beginning of December, finishing in Wellington 60 to 80 days later. This allows both the fast tramper (60 days) or the more moderate tramper (80 days) to reach the South Island when the weather there is still settled, and the rivers are low. The normal range for tramping the South Island is also from 60 to 80 days.

During New Zealand's wet winter and early spring, increased river flows and slippery tracks in the north and, in the south, passes blocked by snow, avalanche danger, and the higher river flows of the spring melt, make tramping Te Araroa inadvisable.

MAP ORIENTATION

The assumption of a north–south through-tramp has also decided the way the maps are laid out in this book. Conventional map presentation puts north at the top, but the maps

ough-trampers Lucy Cant, Alan Householder and Keegan Johnson.

here are aligned as a south-bound tramper would view them, with south at the top and north at the bottom, accurately representing what lies ahead along the direction of travel.

New Zealand has certain defining moments. One of them is to lie in a hot pool at night, under a starry sky, and pick out the Southern Cross. We live under that constellation. It's on our flag. Due south can be ascertained by reference to it. Te Araroa, as a general rule, walks towards it.

LONG WALKS AND SHORT ONES

Long-trail walkers are typically divided into through- and section walkers. Through-walkers do the long trail in a single, sustained tramp. Section walkers aim to complete the trail over time, returning to the trail year upon year.

Te Araroa's through- and section walkers add mana to the trail, but whoever walks it, on whatever smaller distance, also contributes. TAT hopes the stand-alone tracks described in this book will be used by those who want simply a short outing, a day-walk or a two- or three-day stand-alone tramp. Tracks are kept open by people using them and every walker, whether tramping the entire route, or on some smaller section, keeps the trail itself open, and is important to it.

TRAMPING TIPS

If you have not tramped in New Zealand back country before, TAT recommends the Mountain Safety Council courses in bushcraft and river safety. These are available in most New Zealand cities, and smaller centres. River safety is particularly important. New Zealand rivers have short steep catchments, and can rise rapidly. Never attempt to cross a flooding river. Wait, and it will go down.

TAT also recommends that trampers on its more remote sections carry an emergency locator beacon, and that they carry a GPS on those sections, with topographical maps and track line loaded for use. 1:50,000 scale paper maps and a compass should also be carried, in case of GPS malfunction.

New Zealand's Outdoor Safety Code has five further basic tips:

- **Plan your tramp** Plan the route you'll take and the time it's expected to take. Local knowledge is always good, and frequently there'll be a DOC office at the start of major sections with officers who know the territory well.

- **Tell someone** On back-country tracks, tell a reliable mate your route, when you're due out, and when to raise the alarm if you haven't returned. Where intention forms exist at trailheads, fill them in. Similarly, note your arrival, departure, and intentions in the hut books, even if you're not staying there. When you're safely out, make sure your mate knows.

- **Be aware of the weather** New Zealand's weather systems come in very fast, and can be extreme. You must be prepared for any conditions. Rainfall can be heavy, so carry good wet-weather gear and boots, and be prepared for muddy, slippery tracks. Seven-day rainfall forecast maps are available on the Meteorological Service website (see opposite).

- **Know your limits** Challenge yourself within your physical limits and experience.

- **Take sufficient supplies** Make sure you have enough food and equipment in case of delays and any emergency en route. A flooded river is a typical cause of delay, and you should have the ability to wait out its return to a normal flow.

HUTS

Te Araroa walkers intending to use Department of Conservation huts should purchase a back country Hut Pass, available at any DOC visitor and information centre, and at some outdoor sports retailers. Almost every hut on Te Araroa's route is then open to a Hut Pass holder without further payment. The only exception en route is on the Whanganui River, where use of any DOC hut — except Downes Hut way downstream — may require an extra payment. See the DOC website for details. Intending trampers can also purchase separate hut tickets. Most huts en route are single ticket huts. A few are serviced huts with mattresses and other facilities, and these are three-ticket huts. The bivvies en route are free — they're little more than two person shelters. Camping beside the basic back country huts is also free.

You can camp anywhere within the Public Conservation Land back country the trail passes through. If you do, practise no-trace camping. Please do not camp on private land.

TRUE LEFT AND TRUE RIGHT

The tramping notes in this book refer to true left and true right when describing route alongside rivers. The true left bank is the left hand bank when facing downstream. The true right bank is the right hand bank when facing downstream.

HAZARD ZONES

TAT lists three rivers en route, the Waipu, the Rakaia and the Rangitata, as Hazard Zones. The rivers are not part of the trail. The trail stops on their banks, and as Hazard Zones, TAT makes no recommendation to cross on foot. The Hazard Zones are subject to a tramper's own assessments and arrangements for gaining the trailhead on the opposing bank. In every case there is a road bypass around, which is listed in the track notes.

RESPECT

Our landscape is very beautiful. Those fortunate enough to enjoy it do so not just as observers and participants but as kaitiaki — guardians. Kaitiakitanga follows basic environmental principles:

- Leave no trace
- Treat plants and animals with respect
- Carry out all rubbish
- Where toilets are lacking, bury toilet waste at least 50 m from tracks, huts, campsites and water sources
- Take care with fires
- Respect the right of others to enjoy the back country.

KOHA

Te Araroa's construction was a nation-building labour, dedicated to the people of New Zealand for their enjoyment and for the enjoyment of visitors from overseas. Though supported in part by local and central government, the trail remains a citizens' initiative.

The effort to keep Te Araroa open and maintained is substantial. If you're walking the trail and would like to give back to what has been provided freely, then consider making a donation to Te Araroa Trust — this is easily done via the TAT website. Your support will be gratefully received.

USEFUL WEBSITES

Te Araroa Trust	www.teararoa.org.nz
Department of Conservation	www.doc.govt.nz
Meteorological Service	www.metservice.com/national/index
Mountain Safety Council	www.mountainsafety.org.nz

KAURI DIEBACK

Phytophthora taxon Agathis (PTA), aka kauri dieback disease, is having a major impact on New Zealand's forests. In an attempt to control the spread of this disease, some areas of forest have been closed to walkers. As a result, there have been (and will continue to be) necessary amendments and closures to parts of the Te Araroa Trail. For the most up-to-date information, please visit www.teararoa.org.nz/trailstatus/ before you begin any journey on the trail.

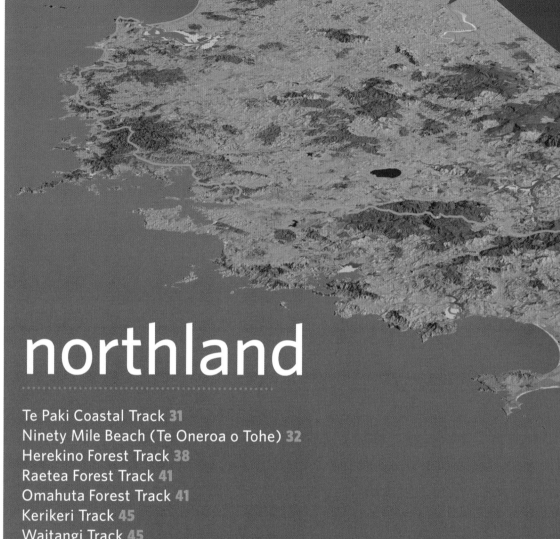

northland

KAURI DIEBACK has resulted in changes/ closures to parts of the trail in this region. Please visit www.teararoa.org.nz/ trailstatus/ for up-to-date information before you begin any journey.

THE LAND

Northland was created by what geologists call obduction — not the usual pliable subduction of tectonic plates returning into the mantle but, as befits what would later be a strong rugby province, one plate going in hard and low against another, and the second plate rising high and collapsing in vast slow-moving avalanches across its opponent. Old oceanic rock lies on top of younger rock, and was uplifted as the plate boundary moved east. This is the justly famous and highly unusual 25–22 million-year-old Northland Allochthon.

This oceanic basalt now holds the Aupouri Peninsula's great sandy sheets of webbing in place. Te Araroa walkers will tread the rock at Cape Reinga, and again on the tracks through the Herekino and Raetea forests. Subsequent uplift has raised rugged hills, which now stand above the plains, too high to farm but draped by old forests. Te Araroa traverses four of those forests in the course of its 120 km Ocean to Ocean Trail, completed in 2011.

The Northland climate is benign, but subject to cyclonic weather bombs from the northeast. The coastlines are long and the rivers short, with myriad feeder streams. Walkers in the north will be untroubled by any of the crossings, except when the rain persists and yesterday's pleasant pool or trickle becomes tomorrow's dangerous torrent.

THE PEOPLE

If tectonic force once overturned the rock of this peninsula, the gradual overturning of tribal Aotearoa by European religion and British law also began here. Missionaries preached the first New Zealand sermons in Northland bays, and a rowdy mix of whalers, adventurers and traders from Australia, at Russell (Kororareka) and Kerikeri, were its first settlers. In 1840 Maori chiefs gathered at Waitangi to debate, and most to sign, the treaty that is this country's founding document. By a simple preamble and three articles, it stated Maori rights, and sanctioned a formal British entry into the country. In 1845 the first anger against the practical implications of that treaty erupted here with the symbolic felling of the British flagpole at Kororareka by Hone Heke, and battles between Maori warriors and British troops.

You'll walk past marae and maybe, by a sweep of the arm, be introduced to tribal rohe wider than any surveyor's cadastral divisions. The north attracts independent people. They build their own dwellings and if they don't all live off the grid, they're forbearing of those who do.

The west coast has long surf beaches, and offers up kai moana to anyone with a boat, a rod, or hands to dig for tuatua. People might shop at Pak'nSave in Kaitaia, but they seem to glean as much from the land and the sea as the commercial marketplace. Sheep, dairy, and beef farmers populate the middle of the peninsula, along with some forestry, and most of the industry in the small towns serves the rural communities. The eastern coast is the region's most prosperous. Orange orchardists and kiwifruit growers around Kerikeri, tourist operators at Paihia, and happy fishermen, retirees, holiday-makers, and sailors within the Bay of Islands live amidst a mosaic of headlands, offshore islands, scalloped bays, and estuaries. A Te Araroa walker enters here onto New Zealand's prettiest coastline.

Hapua and Ratana church.

to Ahipara

145°

N

Ninety Mile Beach

Te Kao

AUPOURI
FOREST

Oromanga Rd

The Bluff

Ninety Mile Beach

AUPOURI
FOREST

Matapia Island

Karatia (Thoms Landing)

Waitiki Landing

Te Paki Stream

Te Paki Station

Scott Point

Te Paki
Coastal Track

Twilight
Beach

Spirits Bay
(Piwhane)

Herangi Hill

Cape Mar
van Dieme

Tapotupotu Bay

Te Werahi Beach

Motuopao Islai

lighthouse

Cape Reinga
(Te Rerengawairua)

START TE ARAROA TRAIL

TE ARAROA STARTS at Cape Reinga lighthouse on the northwestern tip of the North Island. Below the lighthouse is the rocky cape where by legend the spirits of Maori dead slide down the roots of an old pohutukawa tree, beginning an undersea journey to the homeland, Hawaiiki. The site is sacred, and dramatic. Out to sea, the separate currents of the Tasman and Pacific oceans meet in a swirling ocean crease.

A sealed path leads away from the lighthouse before the track turns away to Te Werahi Beach, to the strange mountain of orange that is Herangi Hill and across the soft sandy webbing at the base of the basalt headland, Cape Maria van Diemen. Marker posts lead on and along clifftops of flax and manuka scrub before the track drops down to Twilight Beach (campsite at south end) and then onto a gently rising and entirely pleasant bush-shaded track to Scott Point. Ninety Mile Beach — Te Oneroa o Tohe — stretches away in front to a vanishing point in the south.

The wooden stair takes you four flights down to the beach, and then there's a further hour's walk along the sandy wilderness of Ninety Mile Beach to Te Paki Stream. Through-walkers may want to stop, or go right on. Trampers just in it for the day and awaiting pick-up will have to walk a further 3 km up to the car park on Te Paki Stream Road.

TE PAKI COASTAL TRACK

NORTHERN START	Cape Reinga lighthouse
SOUTHERN END	Te Paki Stream
DISTANCE	20 km
MAPS	1
TRACK STANDARD	Tramping

Cape Reinga lighthouse.

NINETY MILE BEACH (TE ONEROA O TOHE)

NORTHERN START	Te Paki Stream
SOUTHERN END	Ahipara
DISTANCE	80 km
MAPS	2, 3, 4, 5, 6
TRACK STANDARD	Tramping

THE MAORI NAME for Ninety Mile Beach, Te Oneroa o Tohe — the Long Beach of Tohe — remembers an old man's love for his daughter. The aged Ngati Kuri chief set off down the beach, intending to go on past the Hokianga Harbour to see his daughter again before he died, a harsh journey of over 250 km. He did walk the beach, crossed the Hokianga, and kept going, but died just short of his destination.

The walk down Ninety Mile Beach looks easy, but may be harder than you expect. It's certainly flat, but it's natural to choose the hard foreshore over the soft sand above high-tide mark. That foreshore is like concrete, a strain on feet and ligaments. There's no shelter from the sun, and any strong headwind not only slows progress, it can cut you off at the knees, or so it seems, with a disconcerting low-level sand blizzard.

You should filter or treat the water at Te Paki, and beyond. Streams run across the beach and where they do they're attended by a pretty collection of stilts, oystercatchers and godwits. But be aware that the streams can disappear in dry weather. If desperate, track the dry beds back inland and refresh at remnant pools. The campsite at The Bluff does not have piped water or other facilities.

Buses and four-wheel-drive vehicles use the beach. You can see them coming for miles, distorted by distance and afloat on their heat puddle. These apparitions are a first introduction to the beach's mind games. Ninety Mile Beach is so flat and bereft of reference points that flotsam is visible for miles, and impossible to correctly scale or identify until you arrive and get to kick, not the colossal legs of Ozymandias, but a couple of upended fishing crates.

Of all the great walks in New Zealand, this is also the only one that can be easily walked at night. The wind dies, and no roots or rocks can trip you, but the beach may continue its tricks. Changes in colour between wet and dry sand sometimes convince tyro night-hikers that momentarily they're walking downhill, and the white noise of the surf can also add hallucinatory fodder to a blank brain. The dunes to the left and the surf to the right provide ghostly white margins to the night route, and New Zealand's most distinct constellation, the Southern Cross, will be hanging directly in front and beckoning you on. When you reach Hukatere — by daylight is better — the well water is from the depths, and very pure, and there's campsites, showers and supplies for sale.

tt Point Staircase, Ninety Mile Beach.

Rangaunu Harbour

West Coast Rd

to Ahipara

Waipapakauri Beach

Ninety Mile Beach

1

AUPOURI
FOREST

Waiharara

Ninety Mile
Beach

Lake Waiparera

Ninety Mile Beach

Motutangi

Hukatere

1

Hukatere Rd

Houhora Heads

AUPOURI
FOREST

Pukenui

Houhora Harbour

Houhora

Ninety Mile
Beach

Ngataki

1

Ninety Mile Beach

Te Kao

AUPOURI
FOREST

AUPOURI
FOREST

The Bluff

Oromanga Rd

145°

1

AUPOURI
FOREST

N

tion-tramper, Scott Point.

l Schwartz, through-tramper, Ninety Mile Beach.

The long sandy selvedge starts to end around Waipapakauri with its distinctive beach ramp, and a serviced campsite, then beach activity increases through the last 13 km to Ahipara. This settlement of around 1000 was originally a Te Rarawa stronghold, named for a fire kept constantly burning there. It was later bolstered by Yugoslav immigrants working a big gumfield above the settlement, and is now a good place for rest, recreation and resupply.

From here, road-walk to the Herekino Forest Track start.

Ahipara at the end of Ninety Mile Beach.

HEREKINO FOREST TRACK

NORTHERN START	Herekino Saddle on the Kaitaia-Awaroa Rd
SOUTHERN END	Diggers Valley Road or Takahue
DISTANCE	Diggers Valley Road 15 km; Takahue 24 km
MAPS	6, 7
TRACK STANDARD	Tramping

WHEN TE ARAROA workers began work on this track in 2003, they revived old stories of the land. Local Manukau Maori said the Land Information New Zealand maps that name Herekino Forest were wrong; the old name was Orowhana. LINZ listed Herekino Saddle; Maori spoke of a more powerful name, Te Arai — The Door — where spirits pause before their flight up the beach to Cape Reinga. As a result of these talks, Kaitaia kaumatua Don Jack specified 13 pou to assuage spirits and display mana at Te Arai, the track's beginning. Takahue man Peter Griffiths did the carving.

As you enter the forest, those walking south will encounter the first sign of the battle being waged against *Phytophthora taxon Agathis* (PTA), aka kauri dieback disease. The cleaning station here is to ensure all mud is taken off your boots — please take this opportunity to thoroughly clean your footwear, and do so regularly when moving through forests between Cape Reinga and Mt Pirongia to the west of Hamilton.

The track climbs steeply to bracken thickets on the ridge, where you may hear the *u-tick* call of the shy and rare fernbird. The ridge offers glimpses north across the Aupouri Peninsula then descends past Te Araroa's first big kauri. A right-angle turn leads to the Rangiheke Stream, with a cable to grip if the gully becomes slippery.

Two hours in, a signpost alerts you to one of the best kauri groves in Northland, then the track continues along an old forestry road, before returning to forest track, passing disused logging huts, and climbing to the 558 m Taumatamahoe summit. Cellphones work here, and if you allow an hour for a steep, root-crossed descent to Diggers Valley Rd, you can time any pick-up you may have arranged — a necessary step for day-trampers because the exit is a long way from anywhere. Otherwise, camp out, or turn right at Diggers Valley Rd and keep going.

One kilometre south, Te Araroa veers left onto a forestry track through to Waiotehue Road and Takahue. That's a further 9 km. Some through-trampers come from Ahipara in a single day, but it's a very long section.

Kauri tree, Herekino Forest Track.

to Kerikeri

Maungaparerua

Puketolara Rd

Mangakaretu Rd

Mangakaretu Rd

Waiare Rd

Waiare Rd

Puketi Forest HQ

Puketi

PUKETI FOREST

Pirau Ridge

Puketi Rd

Waihou Valley

take right fork

Pukatea Ridge Track

Waipapa River

Waipapa River

Mangapa River

Mangapukahukahu Strm

take right fork

OMAHUTA FOREST

Apple Dam

Rangiahua

Waihou River

take left fork

Omahuta Forest Track

take left fork

Umawera

Jacksons Rd Jn

Omahuta Rd

Omahuta

1

Mangamuka River

Mangamuka

Mangamuka Bridge

1

Mangamuka River

MAUNGATANIWHA

Makene Rd

1

Mangamuka Gorge

RANGE

Take right fork

Pt 727

RAETEA FOREST

Mangataiore

Raetea

Raetea Forest Track

Victoria Valley

Takahue Saddle

Takahue Saddle Rd

Broadwood

1

Takahue Saddle Rd

Warner Rd turnoff

93°

to Kaitaia

Takahue Rd

Takahue

Waiotehue Rd

Diggers Valley

N

FOLLOW TAKAHUE SADDLE RD for 2.5 km alongside the Takahue River until the junction with Warner Rd. Takahue Saddle Rd then turns away from the river. We've started the track and estimated track distances from here because although the forest tramp doesn't begin until the saddle, the old road through to the settlement of Broadwood now sees no vehicles except the odd mountain bike.

The old road climbs steeply through farmland for almost 2 km before it heads into forest at the saddle, then turns left to tread the ascending spine of the Maungataniwha Range. This forest has some of the highest peaks in Northland. They pull down cloud, and the growth is more lush and the tramping more steep and slippery than in the other forests. But high is good, and as the track reaches the Raetea summit (744 m), the views open right out. Northward lies the whole of Muriwhenua, the tail of Maui's fabled fish, Te Ika a Maui, and by local legend the part that guides the destiny of the entire North Island. Southward lies the branching upper reaches of the Hokianga, a harbour dense with Maori lore and early missionary endeavour. Solar-powered cellphone repeaters sit on this highest summit, alongside a useful grassy clearing.

The track then descends before a mild rise to Pt 727. At that junction, one track leads north on a route out to State Highway 1, but Te Araroa continues east for 8.5 km, mainly on old logging roads, and past an old cabin used by long-ago loggers, to exit at a private farm, and from there down Makene Rd to State Highway 1.

Walk via Mangamuka Bridge, which has a pub, a store and a café to the junction of Omahuta and Jacksons roads.

RAETEA FOREST TRACK

NORTHERN START	Takahue Saddle Rd & Warner Rd junction
SOUTHERN END	State Highway 1 at Makene Road
DISTANCE	18.5 km
MAPS	7, 8
TRACK STANDARD	Tramping

FROM THE JUNCTION of Omahuta and Jacksons roads, head east on old forestry roads. Seven hundred metres up from the junction, bear left up Kauri Sanctuary Rd. Vehicles occasionally drive these unmaintained roads, but the grass growing between the tyre tracks confirms they're rare. After 3.5 km there's a junction where Kauri Pa Rd runs off left. That's the one to follow, but if you want to camp, turn right into Kauri Sanctuary Rd and 500 m down the road a green and gold post marks the entrance to a modest campsite with water tank and toilets — Apple Dam. It's a charming spot, with water lilies out on

OMAHUTA FOREST TRACK

NORTHERN START	Jacksons Rd
SOUTHERN END	Puketi Forest Headquarters
DISTANCE	32 km
MAPS	9, 10, 11
TRACK STANDARD	Tramping

the water, and overhung with bush. If you overnight here, you may hear the shriek of kiwi, and certainly you'll hear the eerie cry of the morepork or ruru — New Zealand's bush owl. If you're inclined to detour further, the kauri sanctuary is further down this same road, and Hokianga awaits, the tallest of an impressive bunch. But we digress.

Continue along Kauri Pa Rd a further 1 km, then fork right onto Blackbridge Rd. Stands of young kauri rickers grow on these ridges, but the skinny manuka is the prevailing tree, scenting the air with its myriad white flowers, and attracting the bees, and beekeepers who bring in hives to collect pure manuka honey. Bees stream in and out of two or three such beehive clusters en route, and the bee commerce across the track can look formidable, but the bees are entirely without malice and the trick is simply to button up and walk slowly past.

Keep going to cross a ford, then climb a further kilometre until signposted left onto a soft ridge leading down to Mangapukahukahu Stream. It's a friendly watercourse, but gorgey and subject to flash floods in heavy rain so be careful. Immediately south of the stream's junction with the Waipapa River, a track leads away up the bank, and descends to a shoal that allows a shallow but wet-boots crossing of the main river. Follow the Waipapa upstream for 2.5 km. A track runs parallel to the river for some of the distance, but then it's a wade, knee-deep in places, to the junction with Pukatea Ridge Track.

The track climbs steeply, colonnaded by tall young kauri and tousled below by dracophyllum, then flattens out through an impressive final corridor of mature kauri and a junction with Pirau Ridge Rd. Turn right, and follow this forestry road for 9 km to the Puketi Forest headquarters, where the ranger has a house, and a campground and kitchen awaits.

Walk down Waiare Rd just over 1 km to join the Kerikeri Track.

Raketi Forest, Omahuta Forest Track.

THE TRACK CROSSES Landcorp's Puketotara Farm so an encounter with the farm's heifers, or its Dorset–Romney-cross ewes, is likely. Never put animals in a corner, and when going through a herd of heifers or steers be steadfast but wary.

The track crosses rolling pasture, then leads away to a Mangakaretu Rd walk before re-entering the farm to sidle around Maungaparerua (241 m), a telco hill with cell phone masts and with a wide outlook across the Bay of Islands. The track then traverses a soft ridge, before dropping steeply down to Maungaparerua Stream and entering private farmland. Follow the stream to its junction with the Kerikeri River, follow the river, then cross it on a swing bridge and go on under the highway bridge. A pleasantly grassed track leads through totara groves down to the 27 m Rainbow Falls. A viewing platform overlooks the river's tumble over a lava outcrop here, and the DOC track then leads away through bush and past an old hydro-electric plant 3.5 km to Kerikeri Inlet, the historic Kemp House and the old Stone Store.

The trail then follows the Kororipo Pa track, and local and DOC tracks, through to Pa Rd, from where you'll turn into Kerikeri Inlet Rd. Follow it to the Okura River bridge, ascend the hill beyond and look for a forestry gate marking the start of Te Wairoa Rd, a forestry road.

KERIKERI TRACK

NORTHERN START	Waiare Rd
SOUTHERN END	Kerikeri River car park
DISTANCE	23 km
MAPS	11, 12
TRACK STANDARD	Easy tramping
CLOSURES	April 29–September 14; last weekend in February. Occasional closures during summer for clay mining — consult TAT website.

AS TE WAIROA RD LEAVES Kerikeri Inlet Rd, it ascends gradually through young pines for 2.5 km to a road junction, where you'll veer right onto Skyline Rd, following that for 9 km to Te Puke Rd. At Te Puke Rd, you may like to quickly divert left to see Te Araroa's first-ever track-opening plaque, revealed on February 7 1995. Then Prime Minister Jim Bolger whisked a yellow tarpaulin off a local volcanic stone embedded with lines from A.R.D. Fairburn's poem 'To a Friend in the Wilderness':

> I could be happy, in blue and fortunate weather,
> Roaming the country between you and the sun.

You may wish to add a fern-frond to the Te Araroa cairn standing here, as has become the Te Araroa rite. Otherwise continue east on Te Puke Rd, which will take you out of the forest onto Haruru Falls Rd.

WAITANGI TRACK

NORTHERN START	Te Wairoa Rd
SOUTHERN END	Waitangi Treaty House
DISTANCE	17 km
MAPS	12, 13
TRACK STANDARD	Easy tramping

South of here, the trail follows the same route as the path that once connected the now-vanished Maori village of Okura with Waitangi. It passes Mt Bledisloe, with a short diversion to the summit lookout. A large swathe of land on view from this low summit, including the Treaty Grounds and the Treaty House below, was gifted to the nation in 1932 by a former Governor General, Lord Charles Bledisloe. As a British aristocrat, he perhaps saw more clearly than Pakeha New Zealanders of the time what the Treaty of Waitangi meant to Maori, and the nation. Within two years he'd laid the foundations here for Waitangi's Whare Runanga. That triumvirate of Maori meeting house, Pakeha treaty house and flagstaff were seen by him, and are still seen in New Zealand's more reflective moments, as symbolic of national unity.

The track now descends, with one short road section, to the manicured lawns and the solemn kaitiakitanga that surrounds the place where New Zealand's founding document was signed on 6 February 1840.

Go over Waitangi Bridge past the Te Tii marae, famous as Ngapuhi's host marae for Waitangi Day ceremonies, and on that day a hot spot of debate. Follow the footpath south through to Paihia.

PAIHIA–OPUA COASTAL TRACK

NORTHERN START	Paihia
SOUTHERN END	Opua
DISTANCE	6 km
MAPS	13
TRACK STANDARD	Easy tramping

FOLLOW THE COASTLINE from Paihia around to Haumai Bay — at high tide the alternative is the Seaview Rd footpath. Use the road bridge to cross the Haumai River, then follow the coast again on a high track with good views out onto the Veronica Channel. A boardwalk takes you on through mangroves where you may hear snapping shrimps and see mullet feeding, before continuing around the coast to Opua. A now disused rail line once brought coal from Kawakawa to this port, but the busy boatyards and moorings of a maritime pleasure-boat centre now dominate. Opua is also a car-ferry terminal, with a grocery store and a café catering to yachties.

Long-trail walkers now cross to Waikare. Te Araroa accepts water crossings by whatever means, and a water taxi at Opua will take trampers up the inlet. Local kayaking companies may also provide hire craft — see TAT's website for details. All water transport needs a mid- to high tide to reach Waikare Landing. Otherwise, catch the cross-channel ferry from Opua and walk around from Okiato.

…a crews, Waitangi Day, 2010.

WAIKARE VALLEY RD goes 3 km past the Waikare School and urupa, and Maori farms, to cross the Waikare River on a road bridge. It then narrows into a track and after a further kilometre you must ford the Waikare River. On a good day this is no more than ankle-deep, or you can cross on a concrete pole laid on the riverbed and not get your feet wet. The track ahead runs alongside another watercourse — the Papakauri Stream. This track is a Maori road, a technical term for surveyed access into Maori land blocks which is not public access by right. It was opened to Te Araroa after a series of meetings at Waikare marae. Please treat it with respect.

After 1.5 km the track tails out, and you enter the stream itself for 4 km of shoal- or boulder-hopping, or simply wading through reflective pools overhung with young totara. It'll take you longer than you anticipate, and it shouldn't be attempted during or after heavy rain, but if conditions are right it's a beaut walk.

Russell Forest has been affected by *Phytophthora taxon Agathis* (PTA), aka kauri dieback disease. Te Araroa Trust is working with DOC and local iwi to manage this and work is being done to establish a route clear of the disease. For now though this means that Te Araroa exits Russell Forest earlier than expected.

The stream you've been walking in intersects with the Russell Forest Walkway, and slightly past that junction is a DOC shelter if a stopover point is needed. For the time being, walkers must turn left at that point, onto the walkway, and walk 4.5 km to Russell Road then south on the road 13 km to Helena Bay.

RUSSELL FOREST TRACK

NORTHERN START	Waikare Valley Rd
SOUTHERN END	Junction Punaruku Rd and Russell Rd
DISTANCE	25 km
MAPS	14, 15
TRACK STANDARD	Tramping

FROM RUSSELL RD, head 1 km south on Webb Rd. Just before reaching Teal Bay, on your right, a sign above a gate says you're entering 'High Chaparral'. No sign of a 1970s Western here, though, you're on the farm of the Webb brothers.

Having taken the time to clean boots and equipment at the cleaning station, a short and pleasant walk across the farm will bring you to the start of the uphill climb — first through manuka, then into more established forest.

The track is well-formed and, despite being mainly uphill, makes for enjoyable walking. Towards the top you'll break out into farmland again — move slowly and quietly through livestock if they're present — and cross a

HELENA RIDGE TRACK

NORTHERN START	Junction Russell Rd and Webb Rd
SOUTHERN END	Kaiikanui Rd
DISTANCE	8 km
MAPS	15
TRACK STANDARD	Tramping

few short bush blocks. When you reach another cleaning station be sure to give your footwear another scrub, then it's just a more leisurely wander down the farm track to Kaiikanui Rd.

MOREPORK AND ONEKAINGA TRACKS

NORTHERN START	Kaiikanui Rd
SOUTHERN END	Whananaki
DISTANCE	13 km
MAPS	15, 16
TRACK STANDARD	Tramping

THE TRACK IS WELL FORMED initially, but be careful the coloured markers of predator control don't lead you astray. Stick with the orange triangles, and be aware that past Hansen's Hill, at around the 4 km mark, the track moves sharply to the right and leaves the bench. The track holds that line for a further kilometre before descending beside a boundary fence then climbing sharply to a grassy high point (218 m) that looks out on the coast, and the Poor Knights Islands. This land belongs to the Waetford whanau, so please respect it.

Continue steeply down an old bush track to some pretty little streams before climbing steeply up again. The track then crosses a stile onto a well-formed farm track, turning off after 500 m to pass through a small pine plantation and past a viewpoint close to the Onekainga trig. Follow the fence line along, then down the ridgeline through native bush for 1.5 km, emerging to wide views of the inner Whananaki Estuary. The track descends through the Carson-Harman farm, so please respect it. At the fence between the farm and the treeline, there is another boot-cleaning station — please ensure your footwear is free of mud and debris. For the last 800 m you could encounter Charolais bulls grazing in the fields. Walk slowly alongside the fence and if the bulls start to move, simply wait quietly.

The track emerges onto Whananaki North Rd, and 800 m south along that road, an estuary track takes you through to Whananaki's campground with public toilets and a well-stocked grocery store. Take a stroll along the estuary frontage and you'll see a bit of New Zealand social history. Before the holiday home of the 1970s came the baches of the 1950s. They're built with the simple pragmatism of a hut, gabled miniatures or fibro weekenders, or the single, upwardly slanted roof of the dune-topper, but all with lean-tos added as required, and most with a corrugated-iron water tank weeping a bit of rust beside, and the long-drop behind. Classic.

The Whananaki footbridge — a 350 m marvel — leads across the estuary to Whananaki South.

Kakauri Stream, Russell Forest Track.

Tarawera Track.

TAKE PUKEKAWA RD along the southern shoreline. Beyond Pitokuku Point watch for a grassy track leading away to a stile and onto a disused coach road — now a benched walking track high above an intricate rocky coast. About 3 km into the walk, a short, steep track leads down to the north point of Oruaea Bay. The polished stone column of the *Capitaine Bougainville* memorial names the 16 people lost in 1975, when the blazing freighter was abandoned in an easterly storm. Survivors came ashore near here. There are toilets at Sandy Bay.

Follow the road to Matapouri, then take Clements Rd to the right, and follow it for 2 km.

WHANANAKI COASTAL TRACK

NORTHERN START	Whananaki South
SOUTHERN END	Sandy Bay
DISTANCE	7.5 km
MAPS	16
TRACK STANDARD	Tramping

THE TRACK CLIMBS through private fields to regenerating forest on the hilltop, where local landholders are nurturing kiwi habitat. It enters pine and eucalypt plantations, with glimpses out to the coast, then follows a forest road southeast and down before turning west onto another forest road to pass the kauri giant Tane Moana. The forest continues to a high point with great views up and down the valley, and goes on to an old forestry skid site where a narrow metalled track descends through replanted forest land and pasture to Waiotoi Rd.

Follow the road down to Ngunguru village. Here, locals can ferry you across the estuary — see TAT website for more details — to the Nikau Bay Eco-Camp (accommodation available to walkers) before continuing from there along the quiet and scenic Ngunguru Ford Rd to connect to Mackerel Forest.

MATAPOURI BUSH TRACK

NORTHERN START	Clements Rd
SOUTHERN END	Waiotoi Rd
DISTANCE	10 km
MAPS	17
TRACK STANDARD	Tramping

FROM THE FORESTRY GATE, follow Mackerel Rd downhill through pines. At the bottom of the hill wade the knee-deep Waitangi River, then follow the river bank. The track turns south to cross the Taheke River on a ford, and continues on to meet an old logging track that climbs steeply then descends to a logging gate on Pataua North Rd.

Turn left along Pataua North Rd to Pataua, which has a good serviced campground open in summer. We await a better route across the estuary, but a sea kayaking alternative is also sometimes available from Ngunguru.

MACKEREL FOREST TRACK

NORTHERN START	Ngunguru Ford Rd
SOUTHERN END	Pataua North Rd
DISTANCE	4 km
MAPS	17
TRACK STANDARD	Tramping

TAIHARURU ESTUARY AND KAURI MOUNTAIN TRACK

NORTHERN START	Footbridge, Pataua South
SOUTHERN END	Ocean Beach
DISTANCE	10 km
MAPS	18
TRACK STANDARD	Tramping

THE MANGROVE-FRINGED Taiharuru Estuary is a low-tide route only. Follow Pataua South Rd until it turns inland from the estuary. Cross onto coastal reserve land here and out onto sandy mudflats. Follow around 2.5 km until the white-topped wooden structure on the far side of the estuary is in a direct line from you, then cross. The wade is knee-deep on a slack tide. Break out onto Taiharuru Rd and head south, then turn left into Harambee Rd and follow it up to where it turns into a track across Kauri Mountain. Turn left at the end of this track and follow signage through to Ocean Beach.

Walk south along Ocean Beach, a pleasant walk on white sands with good left and right surf break.

BREAM HEAD TRACK

NORTHERN START	South end Ocean Beach
SOUTHERN END	Urquharts or McLeod beaches, Whangarei Heads
DISTANCE	7 km (Urquharts); 12.5 km (McLeod)
MAPS	18
TRACK STANDARD	Tramping

A SANDY TRACK leads up to Ocean Beach Rd. Follow the road about 1 km to link with DOC's Peach Grove Track and climb to join the Bream Head Track. The Peach Grove Track is steep, and at 200 m elevation bears right to follow the contour, but you can detour left to the Te Whara summit (476 m). The pinnacles here echo the grotesque obelisks on the top of Mt Manaia out to the northwest and the jagged pinnacles of Taranga — the Hen of the Hen and Chickens Islands — out to the east. Beyond the summit are the remnants of Whangarei's World War II defences. The single 5 inch naval gun that once oversaw the harbour fired only three times — never in anger, but with shock waves that knocked down the adjacent ammunition shed.

The through-track goes on through a broadleaf forest that provides food for native birds like tui and kereru, but the birdlife here can include unusual avian visitors from the offshore islands, including the kaka parrot, the red-crowned kakariki and bellbirds. The trail leads across the flank of Mt Lion before dropping steeply down to Urquharts Bay. Te Araroa then becomes a waterfront walk that extends just as far as you need to get a friendly fisherman or boatie to take you across Whangarei Harbour. Good luck, and one tip: recreational fishermen tend to depart boat ramps at Urquharts and Reotahi bays or the jetty at McLeod Bay early morning or evening. There's also a water taxi that operates here — details on TAT's website. The hitchhiking is good into Whangarei city, 30 km distant, for resupply.

Whananaki Coastal Track.

Alex Ward, through-tramper, Whananaki footbridge, Whananaki Coastal Track.

Ocean Beach from the Bream Head Track.

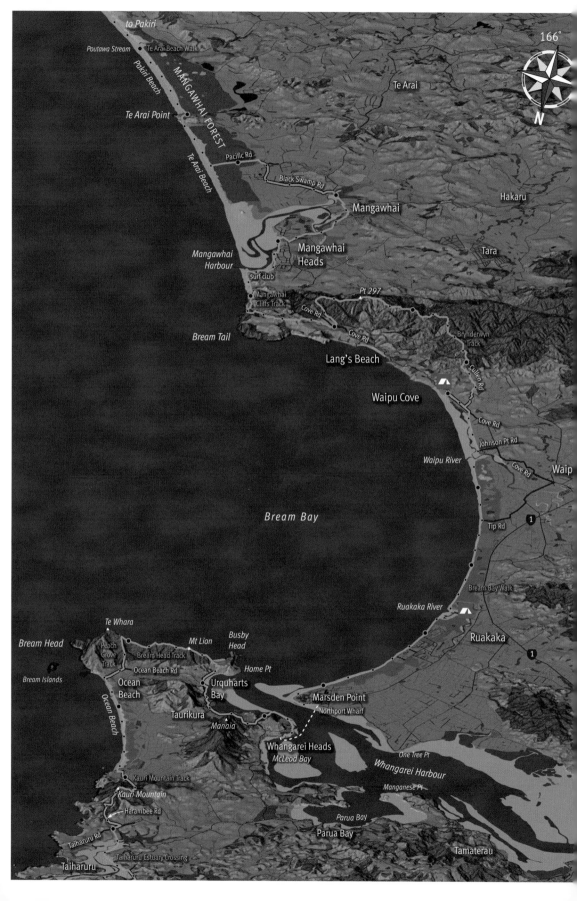

TO AVOID THE high-security area around Marsden Point Wharf, the best landing place is the little beach adjacent to the Northport Wharf. The oil refinery roars and rumbles as you pass, and happy signs dot the fence: *Smile, you are now under closed-circuit surveillance*. It's New Zealand's only oil refinery, opened in 1964 and sited here because of the deep-water port, the flat land and because, unlike a competing site in Wellington, it wasn't a major earthquake risk. No one mentioned tsunamis.

Bream Bay attracts thousands of black-backed gulls, which rise before and settle behind you all the way down to the Ruakaka Estuary, but this brackish inlet attracts wading birds, too. The wrybills, pied stilts, oystercatchers and herons are all interesting waders to watch if you need to wait here, for the estuary is easily crossed only at low tide.

Six km south of Ruakaka an orange post in the dunes marks the Tip Rd road-end. Follow Tip Rd, Uretiti Rd and Nova Scotia Drive to Waipu township, then use the dual-purpose walk/cycleway to take you safely out of town onto Cove Rd. Walk safely on the road shoulder to reach Cullen Rd heading off to the right.

BREAM BAY WALK

NORTHERN START	Marsden Point
SOUTHERN END	Cullen Rd
DISTANCE	23 km
MAPS	18, 19, 20
TRACK STANDARD	Tramping

BRYNDERWYN TRACK

NORTHERN START	Cullen Rd
SOUTHERN END	Cove Rd
DISTANCE	14 km
MAPS	20
TRACK STANDARD	Tramping

FOLLOW CULLEN RD until it turns into a four-wheel-drive track extending 3.5 km to finally pass four private houses on what appears to be their driveway, and intercept DOC's Brynderwyn Hills Walk. The track leads on across a high ridge with wide ocean views to reach a high point at 297 m. The track continues along the ridge before descending to Cove Rd.

Just across Cove Rd, a farm-access road leads away uphill for 1 km then follows a marked and stiled route 2 km across farmland to link with the Mangawhai Cliffs Track.

MANGAWHAI COASTAL WALKWAY

NORTHERN START	North end, Mangawhai Cliffs Track
SOUTHERN END	Mangawhai Surf Club
DISTANCE	3.5 km
MAPS	20
TRACK STANDARD	Easy tramping

THIS TRACK IS benched into the high flank of a coastal escarpment. It's one of New Zealand's top coastal walks — elevation, a good track surface colonnaded by nikau palms, and out to sea the Hen and Chickens Islands and the formidable Sail Rock. Taranga — the Hen — is a 17 million-year-old volcanic remnant but the Chickens are New Zealand's ancient basement rock, greywacke. This solves the old conundrum — the Chickens came first, not the egg. Further out lies Little Barrier Island — Hauturu — a separate volcanic eruption from 1.5 million years ago, and now New Zealand's oldest bird sanctuary.

The track descends past a lookout to the beach where you'll find other evidence of New Zealand's volcanoes. Near the surf club, the intricately weathered grey rock on the cliffs is volcanic dacite, whose successive, long-ago oozing onto the sea floor gives it an unusual layered construction. Amidst the tidal wrack on this beach, the observant may sometimes find small pieces of dense pumice, effusions from the undersea 'black smokers' along the Kermadec Trench.

Walk through Mangawhai and across the estuary bridge to Black Swamp Rd. Follow along to Pacific Rd and turn onto Te Arai Beach.

ngawhai Cliffs Coastal Track.

bby McColl, section-tramper, Pakiri Beach, Te Arai Beach Walk.

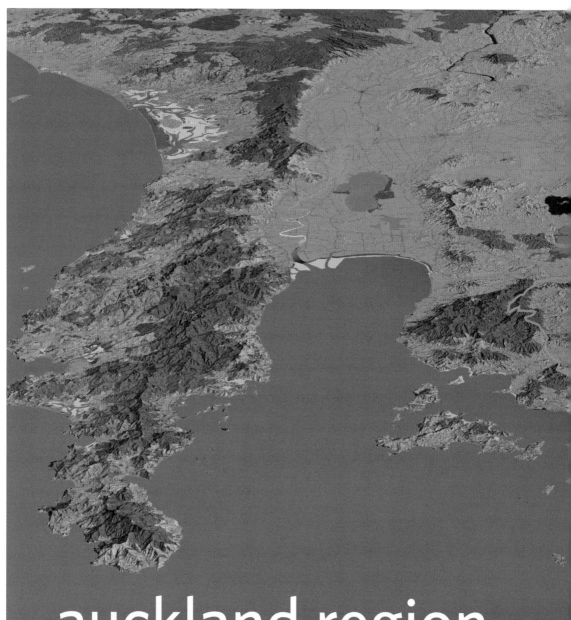

auckland region

KAURI DIEBACK has resulted in changes/closures to parts of the trail in this region. Please visit www.teararoa.org.nz/trailstatus/ for up-to-date information before you begin any journey.

THE LAND

The estuaries become more intricate and the islands pack more closely together as you approach Auckland city. From Pakiri Beach at night, New Zealand's largest city is already a glow behind the hills, and from Mt Tamahunga, still 100 walking kilometres distant, you can spot the Sky Tower. Puhoi is the last independent settlement, its rolling farmland pleasantly patched with bush, and then you're into city outskirts, walking beside the soft sandstone cliffs of the region.

The appearance of Rangitoto (260 m), an extinct volcano that's just 600 years old, is the first hint that Auckland sits astride a volcanic field. The Tamaki isthmus is passing slowly across a hot spot in the earth's mantle, and for 250,000 years the land has boiled like a pot of old porridge. Explosion craters, scoria cones and shield volcanoes pock the landscape, most pleasantly grassed now, their craters and tuff rings rounded by time. Te Araroa treads the summits of two such green volcanoes.

Further south, the Hunua Ranges shadow the city. Big, patient, not unduly high, they supply Auckland with over half its water.

THE PEOPLE

Within weeks of signing the Treaty of Waitangi on February 6 1840, Lieutenant Governor Hobson sailed into the Waitemata Harbour aboard HMS *Herald* and ran his eye over the isthmus of Tamaki Makaurau. Green humps ashore that might compare to the seven hills of Rome. An ocean each side, and a potential port on each. Major rivers snaking inland.

Omaha, with Auckland on the horizon.

Ngati Whatua as mana whenua and eager sellers. Also, the benign symmetry of the volcanic island at the harbour entrance — Rangitoto. A new colony needs a capital city and this could be the site.

Within months, quite separately from this government expedition, and acting on a tip-off, a canny 22 year-old Scottish doctor, with his business partner, buys up nearby Browns Island and waits for the Crown to return. His hunch is right. The deed of sale to the Crown goes through on September 18 that year, and the opportunities are immediate. Land speculation. Timber. Grog. Insurance. Banking. Sir John Logan Campbell would become Auckland's first mayor.

As it began, so it goes on. Wellington took away Auckland's capital city status in 1865, but she has remained the queen city of commerce. One third of New Zealanders live here, and over 300,000 of those are Pacific Islanders or Maori, allowing the claim, if you're so inclined, that Auckland is the biggest Polynesian city in the world. It's also home to most of New Zealand's Asians, and to smaller immigrant groups.

Auckland has never been as civic-minded as New Zealand's other cities. Its beginnings were not as unitary, its geography not as contained. It sprawls, but sprawl is also commodious. Aucklanders built upon large sections, and even with infill housing the city's interior remains shaded by an urban forest and greened by large parks. Out on the edges, the Hauraki Gulf islands and the dozens of east and west coast beaches have laid a further calming hand upon this population and opened it to the outdoors — to surfing, sailing, swimming, to all the rituals of the beach, and to the barbecues of summer.

ONE KILOMETRE FROM THE BEACH entry there's a significant stream crossing. Beyond that the track crosses Te Arai Point and descends again to Pakiri Beach. You'll often see wet-suited figures on the waves, and horse riders on the sand, the main users of this special white beach that squeaks. Unlike most sand, which has a shell base, Pakiri sand is infinitesimal particles of quartz, milled round like tiny marbles and flowing like water from your hand. As to the squeak — it's either the particles rubbing together under the force of your kick, or the air escaping from between the impelled particles. Either way, it's part of the fun on this beach.

Poutawa Stream crossing is 5 km on from Te Arai Point, and the wide, wet fan of the Pakiri River mouth is 7 km beyond that. Cross it to reach the Pakiri campground.

Walk up Pakiri River Rd to the crossroads, and go straight ahead into Bathgate Rd.

TE ARAI BEACH WALK

NORTHERN START	Pacific Rd road-end
SOUTHERN END	Pakiri River Rd beach Access
DISTANCE	17 km
MAPS	22
TRACK STANDARD	Easy tramping

THE TRACK GOES OVER Mt Tamahunga (437 m), the highest Te Araroa summit between Auckland and Whangarei. The track is named for Te Kiri, a Ngati Wai chief who in 1864 rescued 180 Waikato prisoners from Governor George Grey's nearby Kawau Island and brought them to secluded freedom here. It was impregnable country, and the government of 1864 chose simply to plead for their return. It was met with the reply: 'How many birds, having escaped the snare, return to it?'

From Bathgate Rd, head up steep farm pasture for 2.5 km to the ridge. The track goes through farmland then bush for a climb to the summit including a 'Hillary Step' hacked out of the stone. Immediately above the step is a lookout. Savour the view of blue headlands receding north to Bream Head, because the summit itself is enclosed in bush.

A chopper platform provides a good lunch spot, then the track descends to Matakana Valley Rd through beautiful regenerating native bush.

TE HIKOI O TE KIRI

NORTHERN START	Bathgate Rd
SOUTHERN END	Matakana Valley Rd
DISTANCE	11 km
MAPS	23
TRACK STANDARD	Tramping

DOME FOREST TRACK

NORTHERN START	Govan Wilson Rd
SOUTHERN END	Dome Tearoooms
DISTANCE	12.5 km
MAPS	23, 24
TRACK STANDARD	Tramping

FOLLOW THE CLAY four-wheel-drive track and respect the privacy of the house alongside. One kilometre into the tramp, Conical Peak Rd heads left, but take the right fork, and continue uphill 1.5 km to a signed turnoff left into the forest. The track descends into the valley, crosses the Waiwhiu Stream then uses forest roads, climbing to the ridgeline of DOC's Dome Forest and following along 5 km, past a grove of mature kauri, to the Dome trig. The summit is enclosed by bush and you have to climb the trig to get the view. The track down is steep, then it is a well-maintained walking track with terrific view points out to the eastern coast. and the Dome Tearooms is a happy watering spot to finish.

MOIRS HILL TRACK

NORTHERN START	Dome Tearooms
SOUTHERN END	J Tolhopf Rd
DISTANCE	18 km
MAPS	24
TRACK STANDARD	Tramping

THE TRACK IS MIXED GRADE, with back roads and a brief passage down a sealed highway, but Moirs Hill (357 m) remains a visible goal throughout much of it. Cross State Highway 1 and follow Kraak Rd to a forestry gate at the road-end. Follow the forestry road 1 km before taking a left to an old skid site. Cross into native bush within DOC's Smyth Reserve and then go via Smyth Rd to Kaipara Flats Rd, up a private driveway, avoiding the house, and across the farm. Two further back roads take you into Matthew Rd, which is gated at the end, and turns into a track up Moirs Hill. Just beyond the Moirs summit, the track leads steeply downhill, ending at Ahuroa Rd. J Tolhopf Rd is straight ahead. Follow it down a further kilometre to the marked entrance gate of Dunns Track.

DUNNS TRACK

NORTHERN START	J Tolhopf Rd
SOUTHERN END	Ahuroa Rd
DISTANCE	3 km
MAPS	24, 25
TRACK STANDARD	Tramping

THE TRACK ROUTE WAS GIFTED by prominent local farmers and conservationists, Val and the late Arthur Dunn. Follow the markers to enter onto a wide, grassy track through part of Dunns Bush — covenanted by the QEII National Trust. The track opens out to farmland and a sugarloaf rock, with a stiled access if you want to linger. The trail goes on down through farmland to end at the Remiger Rd junction with Ahuroa Rd.

Hikoi o Te Kiri leading to Tamahunga summit.

Trampers Fiona Mackenzie and Mark Tillett, Waiwhiu Stream, Dome Forest Track.

THE TRACK crosses the Puhoi River and ascends to a ridge, which it follows through stands of native bush with giant pūriri, totara and kauri abundant. Native bush becomes pine forest and then farmland, with wonderful views of the valley below — which are even more enjoyable if the autumn colours are out. The town below has a special history, founded in 1893 by 83 German-speaking immigrants from Bohemia. They remained isolated and self-reliant for many years and today's town retains much of that character, charm, composure and Catholicism. You look down on a hamlet cupped in a sacralised valley — complete with beer garden opposite the track end.

You can hire a kayak at the village and paddle the 7 km down the river. Puhoi means slow water, and the paddle through to Wenderholm Regional Park is easy, but does cost money and is tide dependent.

PUHOI TRACK

NORTHERN START	Ahuroa Rd
SOUTHERN END	Puhoi
DISTANCE	9 km
MAPS	25
TRACK STANDARD	Tramping

JOIN THE PERIMETER TRACK out of Wenderholm, exiting to cross the Waiwera road bridge and walking through to Waiwera, where there's a store, hot pools, a campground and a bistro. From Waiwera it's an easy low-tide rock-hop along the coast to Hatfields Beach. The route onward to Orewa Beach is low tide also, again on rock platforms, but if you miss the tide you can still get through by taking the public walkway at the south end of Hatfields.

South of Orewa, take the bridge across the river, then the path under the main road and along a pleasant walkway around the Orewa Estuary. The route then threads its way through Silverdale and past the historic Wade Tavern, before following the road shoulder to Stillwater.

The Okura Bush Walkway leads off from Duck Creek Rd, and follows shoreline then an overland route 3 km to Dacre Cottage. The cottage was built in 1855 by Henry Dacre, reputedly from bricks that were ballast from his father's trans-Tasman sailing vessel. It's been restored by history buffs using the traditional mortise-and-peg system instead of nails on the rafters, and timber shingles on the roof. Beyond lies Dacre Point, and beyond that, the mouth of the Okura Estuary. On the far side of the estuary, the pale cliffs of Piripiri Point slope down to a beach. You need to get to that beach, and that's doable, but only at low tide.

HIBISCUS COAST WALK

NORTHERN START	Wenderholm Regional Park
SOUTHERN END	Okura Estuary
DISTANCE	30 km
MAPS	25
TRACK STANDARD	Tramping

The estuary is hip-deep at the fourth white marker in from the mouth at low tide, and when the tide's slack, there's no current to worry you. This is a Hazard Zone, without recommendation from TAT, and subject to your own assessment and skills. An alternative road route around to the Long Bay Regional Park is listed on the website.

AKARANA TRAIL (NORTH SHORE COASTAL WALK)

NORTHERN START	Piripiri Beach
SOUTHERN END	Devonport
DISTANCE	23 km
MAPS	26, 27
TRACK STANDARD	Easy tramping

YOU'VE NOW HIT metropolitan Auckland, treading a green route through Long Bay Regional Park, and entering urban footpath alongside the Marine Education and Recreation Centre. The walk knits in clifftop paths alongside houses that face onto the Hauraki Gulf views, and descends to easy wave-platform progress beneath cliffs where bits of debris blind-tap their way down. The cliffs erode backwards and the architecture advances forwards. It's a happy entrance onto the city.

The world's long trails do not go through cities but Te Araroa does, under the catchcry 'When you're in New Zealand you're in New Zealand all day'. New Zealand flat white coffees — you'll get them at Browns Bay. New Zealand ice cream — Browns Bay again. New Zealand pretensions — the faux rock covering of the old waterfront sewer pipe between Murrays Bay and Mairangi Bay. New Zealand yachts — try Takapuna or just about anywhere. Devonport makes a good stopping point. It's the city's old maritime and naval centre and the main street is appropriately Victorian. At Windsor Park beside the ferry wharf, there's a Te Araroa stone with a stanza by poet C.K. Stead that condenses much of what the locals call, simply, 'The Shore':

Footprints in sand, a light wind at the door,
Tides, ferries, the bridge, and always islands
Floating in blue, or sunk in a stone composure . . .

Take the ferry across the harbour to the isthmus.

ough-trampers Lane Schaffer, Dennis Behan and Alice Smith on the North Shore Coastal Walk.

kland from North Head.

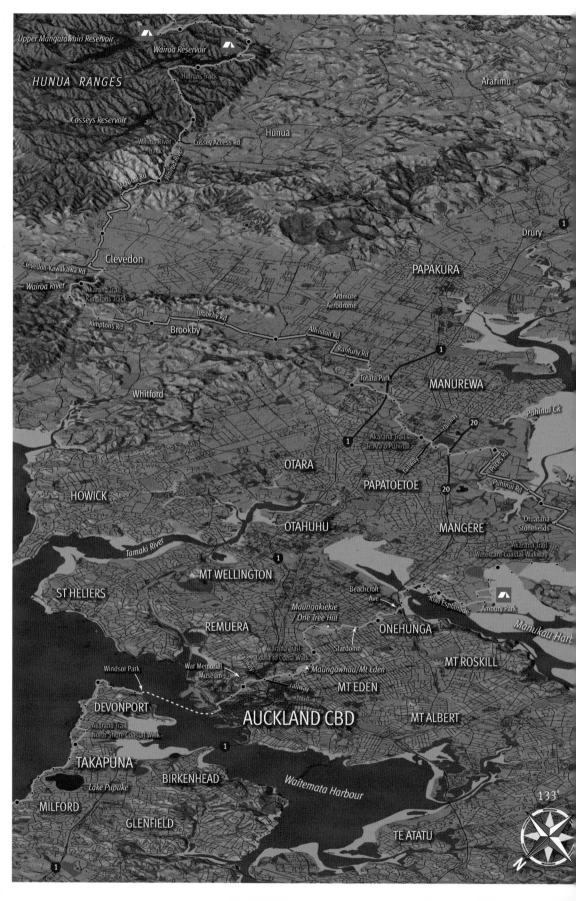

Upper Mangatāwhiri Reservoir

Wairoa Reservoir

HUNUA RANGES

Hunuas Track

Cosseys Reservoir

Ararimu

Wairoa River Track

Cossey Access Rd

Hunua

Mt Wiroa Rd

Wairoa River

Clevedon

Drury

1

PAPAKURA

Clevedon-Kawakawa Rd

Wairoa River

Akarana Trail
Kimptons Track

Ardmore
Aerodrome

Kimptons Rd

Brookby Rd

Brookby

Alfriston Rd

Ranfurly Rd

1

Whitford

Totara Park

MANUREWA

Puhinui Ck

1

railway

20

Akarana Trail
Te Ara o Puhinui

OTARA

railway

Prices Rd

Puhinui Rd

At

HOWICK

PAPATOETOE

20

MANGERE

Otuataua
Stonefields

OTAHUHU

Akarana Trail
Watercare Coastal Walkway

Tamaki River

MT WELLINGTON

1

Beachcroft
Ave

Kiwi Esplanade

Ambury Park

ST HELIERS

Maungakiekie
/ One Tree Hill

ONEHUNGA

Manukau Hart

REMUERA

Stardome

MT ROSKILL

Akarana Trail
Coast to Coast Walk

railway

Windsor Park

War Memorial
Museum

Maungawhau/Mt Eden

DEVONPORT

Akarana Trail
North Shore Coastal Walk

railway

MT EDEN

MT ALBERT

AUCKLAND CBD

1

TAKAPUNA

BIRKENHEAD

Waitemata Harbour

133

Lake Pupuke

MILFORD

GLENFIELD

TE ATATU

N

THE COAST TO COAST WALK is signposted through Auckland's central business district by distinctive orange signs with white arrows and Te Araroa's logo tucked in one corner. This is the heart of the original city, and some of Auckland's oldest villas line the early route, alongside military remnants from the 1840s. The University of Auckland campus still preserves a section of defensive wall from the early British Fort Britomart. The Auckland War Memorial Museum and the Stardome Observatory are en route, as are two volcanic summits, Mt Eden (Maungawhau) and One Tree Hill (Maungakiekie), each one sufficiently high to overlook the Auckland CBD and the entire urban isthmus.

Maori called this isthmus Tamaki Makaurau — Tamaki of a thousand lovers. The isthmus pa were some of the biggest in Aotearoa, each a locus of vital resources and tribal battle. Maungawhau was named for the whau tree's very light wood, which was used for net floats, and Maungakiekie for the kiekie plant whose bracts provided food. The tomb of the city's first mayor, the revered Sir John Logan Campbell, is inscribed in Latin on top of One Tree Hill: *Si monumentum requiris, circumspice.* ('If you want my monument, look around you.')

Auckland is a city of separate centres, and after leaving the CBD and the old historical centre, the track passes close to three of the embedded villages, Parnell, Mt Eden and Onehunga. When you reach Onehunga Bay you'll have crossed from the Pacific Ocean to the Tasman Sea.

AKARANA TRAIL (COAST TO COAST WALK)

NORTHERN START	Ferry Building
SOUTHERN END	Onehunga Bay
DISTANCE	16 km
MAPS	27
TRACK STANDARD	Easy tramping

HEAD DOWN BEACHCROFT AVE to the footbridge across the motorway, then follow Orpheus Drive along the foreshore. This leads to the old Mangere Bridge, relegated to bike and foot traffic only after its footings broke through the lava crust and left it with a somewhat sway back. Head right into Kiwi Esplanade and follow it to Ambury Park. The campground there has fresh water on tap, loos and a barbecue. You must book ahead for this camp — see TAT's website for details.

Link to the Watercare Coastal Walk along the Manukau shoreline. It passes roost islands where you may spot godwits, lesser knots, wrybills or the distinctive at-arms slope of the oystercatcher's red bill. It passes Watercare's sewage treatment plant, a modern ultraviolet cleansing facility that is, when it releases its sterilised fluids into the harbour on the outgoing tide at 25 cumecs

AKARANA TRAIL (MANUKAU SECTION)

NORTHERN START	Onehunga Bay
SOUTHERN END	Clevedon
DISTANCE	52 km
MAPS	28, 29, 30
TRACK STANDARD	Tramping

a second, the source of Auckland's biggest river.

The track goes alongside the Otuataua Stonefields — former Maori gardens that used sun-warmed rock to extend their seasons — then on streets past Auckland Airport and down to Te Ara o Puhinui, a track that follows the Puhinui Stream. With occasional footpath deviations, this track then follows the stream up to the Auckland Botanic Gardens and out to Kimptons Rd with one unpleasant 6 km road-shoulder walk along Brookby Rd linking to Kimptons Track, with great views across the Wairoa River and the eastern coast, then through Clevedon Reserve into Clevedon township.

Walk out of Clevedon on the Clevedon–Kawakawa Bay Rd footpath, turn right onto McNicol Rd and follow through to the road-end and link to the 4 km Wairoa River Track along the Wairoa River. This brings you through to the Hunua Ranges Regional Park.

HUNUAS TRACK

NORTHERN START	Cossey Access Rd
SOUTHERN END	Lyons Rd
DISTANCE	31 km
MAPS	30, 31
TRACK STANDARD	Tramping

SEVEN HUNDRED METRES up Cossey Access Rd, enter the Cossey Gorge Track, join to the Massey Track, then follow along the ridgeline to the Wairoa Dam, one of four large reservoirs in the Hunuas. The track leads on another 5 km via the Wairoa Loop track and Repeater Rd to a basic campsite with a composting toilet. It continues south via Moumoukai Rd, until it passes close to the Upper Mangatangi Dam campsite, 17 km into the tramp. This section of the park is set aside for mountain-biking, but there's plenty of room for joint use.

Follow along to Moumoukai Valley Rd. The road has an old ford across the Milne Stream that's been washed out, but it's usually easily crossed and the road leads on to the Lower Mangatawhiri campsite. The track then crosses the Mangatawhiri River, also usually quite wadeable here, then heads steeply uphill to Pt 445 and continues along the ridge before a steep descent to a swing bridge across the Mangatawhiri River. The track stays in bush looking out over farmland, before crossing onto the farm to exit at the Lyons Rd road-end. (See map on page 80 for that end.)

Walk down Lyons Rd, and along State Highway 2 to the Mangatawhiri road bridge.

ner of Queen and Wellesley streets, Auckland.

iroa Reservoir, Hunuas Track.

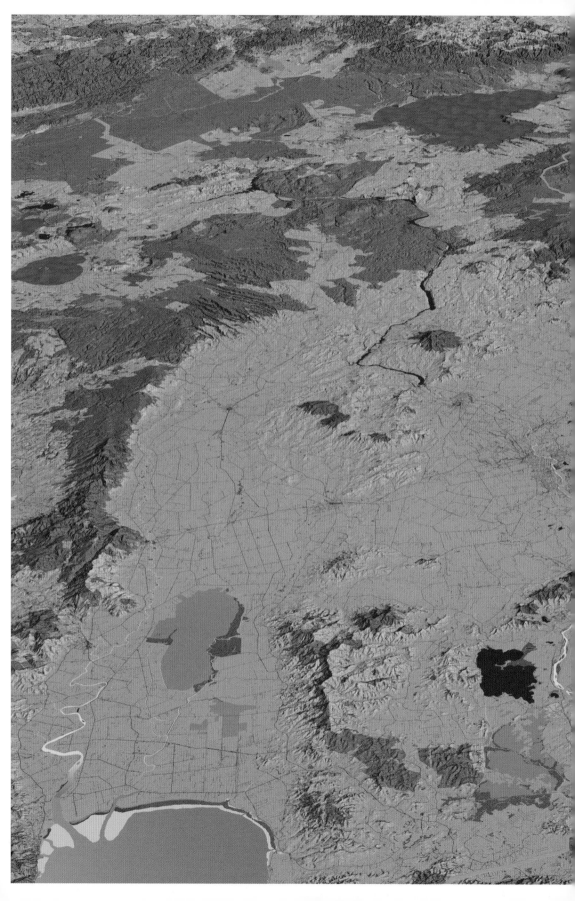

waikato-
king country

THE LAND

Some of the world's youngest and most violent explosion craters lie to the southeast. You won't easily recognise them, because many of the destructive calderas are now low-lying lakes or ranges of volcanic domes, but material from successive pyroclastic flows — the ground-hugging billows that radiate swiftly from collapsing volcanic plumes — still mantle the region. One of Te Araroa's first Waikato tracks is marked by a 1 tonne ignimbrite boulder, a type of rock first named by a New Zealand geologist after studies in this region. Ignimbrite is formed by pyroclastic flows maintaining temperatures and densities that weld pumice and ash into rock.

Waikato's dairy farms now populate these rich volcanic soils, and the scorched earth of these past cataclysms has turned bright green. The Waikato — New Zealand's mightiest river — runs through it all, rising at the Central Plateau and discharging into the Tasman Sea. The river too has bent its knee to the ferocity of ancient eruptions, changing course 26,000 years ago from its outlet on the eastern coast, and now filling eight hydro dams en route to its discharge into the Tasman Sea.

West of the river and beyond the volcanic crags of Pirongia, limestone country announces itself with distinctive karst hills, pale bluffs, underground cave systems, and white limestone fill on farm driveways and races. In the distance, always visible from high points right through the region, lie the volcanic mountains of the Central Plateau.

THE PEOPLE

The Waikato Maori had a saying for their river: *He piko, he taniwha* — at every bend a chief. Numerous kainga lined the riverbanks. Waikato Maori initially adapted well to the settler culture in Auckland, bringing in supplies and setting up their own mills and trading enterprises. Concern at the rapid loss of Maori land to settler purchases led to inter-tribal meetings and the inauguration of Tainui Chief Potautau Te Wherowhero as Maori King in 1858. The British saw the King Movement as a direct threat. The commerce between Auckland city and the Waikato fell away, and British troops invaded the Waikato in 1863, forcing the Kingites into exile in what became known as the King Country. Huge swathes of Waikato land were confiscated by the Crown, and reparations have only recently been made.

The trail follows the river to Huntly, a coal town, runs across the Hakarimatas and descends on Ngaruawahia township and Turangawaewae, Tainui's great riverside marae, and home to the present Maori King Tuheitia Paki. Just upstream is Hamilton, the Waikato's proud river city, and its main industrial and service centre. The trail follows a green route through the city before exiting at Dinsdale to cross dairy land alongside the Waipa River, then climb Pirongia, a challenging peak and a serious tramp.

Beyond, Waitomo is famous for its glow-worm caves. Adventure companies have developed various abseiling and blackwater rafting adventures within the labyrinth underground. King Country farmers have generously allowed Te Araroa access through the karst country to Te Kuiti, and the trail then moves into the bush-clad enormity of the Hauhungaroa Forest. (Hunters use the Hauhungaroa tracks and huts, so don't wear your antler hat.) The trail then emerges close to the Central Plateau, where trampers again predominate on a network of mountain trails.

milton city with the Waikato River.

THE TRACK ALONG the Mangatawhiri stopbank overlooks an unusual polder-style agriculture — crop and dairy lowlands protected by dykes and drained by pumps. From the State Highway 2 bridge, follow the stopbank 5 km until it's crossed by a drainage ditch. The swamp on the far side is duck-hunters' territory. It's a small corner of one of New Zealand's largest swamplands, the Whangamarino.

The stopbank turns at right angles to reach an Archimedes screw at the MacIntyre Rd road-end. As you follow the road out, the high ground to the left is an old battleground, the Koheroa Ridges. On July 12 1863, 500 British troops under General Duncan Cameron crossed the Mangatawhiri into Waikato territory and dug redoubts on this high ground. Maori dug trenches across the ridges in front to block the British Army's route south. The first battle of the Waikato war loomed.

At the end of MacIntyre Rd turn right into Kellyville Rd, cross the railway line and follow a bush track, under two motorway bridges and on between the motorway and the river into Mercer. The town used to be an important rail stop, its refreshments once immortalised, in a parody of Shakespeare's famous line, as 'The squalid tea of Mercer is not strained'. It's now an equally hospitable motorway stopover, with pub, cheese shop, McDonald's and a coffee shop.

As you move out of town you'll pass a strange New Zealand memorial. The iron turret by which the names of Mercer's World War I and World War II dead are remembered is from the river gunboat *Pioneer* — symbol of another war altogether, one fought on this very doorstep.

MANGATAWHIRI TRACK

NORTHERN START	State Highway 2 bridge, Mangatawhiri
SOUTHERN END	Mercer
DISTANCE	10 km
MAPS	32
TRACK STANDARD	Tramping

TWO SHORT SECTIONS within this longer track make good walks in themselves. The track between Skeet Rd and Oram Rd is historically interesting, for it reaches the old Te Teoteo pa, end-point of the 1863 battle for the Koheroa Ridges, and also the Whangamarino Redoubt, built by the British beside the pa. It's an easy 3 km day-walk. The 9 km track from Drag Way to the Te Kauwhata pumphouse is a good river track, with road access either end.

From Mercer, cross the overhead motorway bridge. Skeet Rd turns away right and the track climbs to overlook road and rail corridors, and the river. In 1863, Cameron's troops charged down the Koheroa Ridges and

WAIKATO RIVER TRACK (MERCER TO RANGIRIRI SECTION)

NORTHERN START	Mercer
SOUTHERN END	Rangiriri
DISTANCE	27 km
MAPS	32, 33
TRACK STANDARD	Tramping

overwhelmed Maori fighters, but you won't easily pick these ridges, for they loop distantly east before closing back on Te Teoteo pa. A British redoubt is still plainly visible on the right, however, a plum-pudding shape between the northbound and southbound motorway lanes. Maori lost 30 warriors including their chief Te Huirama on the ridges, before abandoning the fight and the pa. General Cameron lost one soldier. His troops built the Whangamarino Redoubt alongside the pa, and wheeled up Armstrong guns to shell the new Maori defensive line at Meremere.

For three months Cameron stayed put. Maori guerrillas picked away behind, at his supply lines and at south Auckland settlers, but by October, Cameron had brought in from Australia two river gunboats, the *Pioneer* and the *Avon*, and four armoured barges to haul 600 troops upriver. Meremere Maori had only a couple of ship's guns to stop this armada steaming through. Outflanked, they fell back to the next defensive position at Rangiriri.

From the old redoubt, the track descends to Oram Rd, ducks under three bridges, and follows the river a further 5 km to Drag Way. An ignimbrite boulder here marks the 2001 opening by Sir Edmund Hillary of this early Te Araroa link, and carries a verse from the Topp Twins song 'Turangawaewae':

A sacred place to be
By the banks of the mighty Waikato
As she flows out to the sea

The next 9 km to the Te Kauwhata pumphouse on Churchill East Rd has good vantage points above the river. You also get close to the water here. Huge goldfish — koi carp — raise fat and wordless lips from the shallows as you go by, and that, in mimicry, is the Waikato's great and secret charm: the utter silence as its mighty tonnages of fresh water slip by. The 9 km onward from the pumphouse to Rangiriri is mainly flat, and uses the stopbank, parallel to the road.

kato River and Motutawa Island from the Waikato River Track (Mercer to Rangiriri).

mper Jeremy Toth crossing Mangatawhiri Stream.

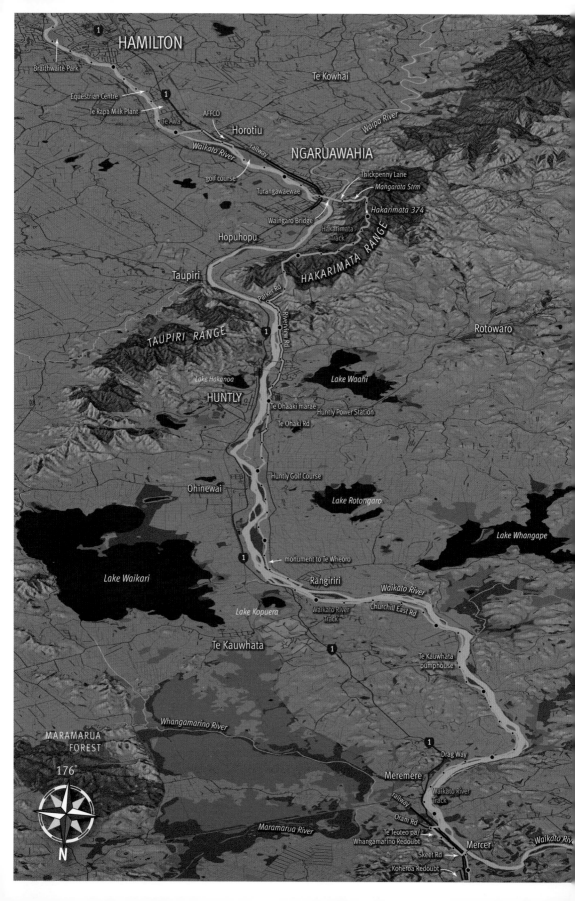

CROSS THE WAIKATO from Rangiriri on the road bridge, and a stile takes you onto stopbanks on the true left of the Waikato. The chimneys of the Huntly Power Station stand as orange-topped pillars in the distance. One and a half kilometres on from the stile, a monument to Te Wheoro recalls a Ngati Naho chief and a life torn between loyalty to the Crown and loyalty to Maori. Te Wheoro argued in the 1850s against appointing a Maori King. Later he helped broker the return of the exiled Maori King Tawhiao to Ngaruawahia in 1881. In 1884, disillusioned that the government he'd supported had not dealt fairly with Waikato, he travelled with the Maori King to London to seek redress from Queen Victoria for the land seizures.

At 7 km, the track comes up to the Huntly Golf Course, kept safe from the 16th fairway's golf balls by a screen of trees. The clubhouse is close by and open most weekends for hot food, maybe even a beer. Walkers welcome.

The track follows the stopbank out to Te Ohaki Rd to circumvent the Huntly Power Station's ash ponds, then returns to the stopbank, crossing Maori land between Te Ohaaki marae and the river. For the last 200 m it enters bush to finish at Huntly Power Station, a fine piece of 1970s brutalist architecture and New Zealand's largest thermal power plant. A carved bas-relief taniwha here guards Dame Te Atairangikaahu's blessing upon Te Araroa walkers:

Kia tupato kia pai to hikoi — Walk the path in safety
Me te titiro whanui kia koa — Look deeply and learn
Ki nga taonga kei mua i a koe — From your surroundings

In the sculpture park beyond is an immense modernist Maori figure with poupou, standing up from a reflective pool. It embodies Tainui's anger at the raupatu of 1865 and its proud resolution, the Crown's condign Deed of Settlement of 1995, signed by the then Maori Queen.

Walk out to the Hakarimata Track on Riverview Rd and turn into Parker Rd.

WAIKATO RIVER TRACK (RANGIRIRI TO HUNTLY SECTION)

NORTHERN START	Rangiriri
SOUTHERN END	Huntly
DISTANCE	16 km
MAPS	33, 34
TRACK STANDARD	Easy tramping

HAKARIMATA TRACK

NORTHERN START	Parker Rd, Huntly
SOUTHERN END	Ngaruawahia
DISTANCE	11 km
MAPS	34, 35
TRACK STANDARD	Tramping

THE TRACK CLIMBS through stands of rimu to the Upper Lookout, with views north across Huntly township, and the river receding north. Taupiri Mountain, Tainui's solemn urupa, its summit reserved for Maori kings and queens, is an occluded presence out to the east. Then the forest closes around and the track undulates for some hours across the main ridge to the Hakarimata Trig at 374 m. Two hundred metres beyond the trig, a track leads left towards the Mangarata Stream, down onto Brownlee Ave, through to the Waingaro Bridge over the Waipa River. From there, through-walkers can take a hard left onto Sampson St to go around the river, under Great South Rd and south. Or continue straight ahead on Waingaro Rd to reach the Ngaruawahia main street.

TE AWA

NORTHERN START	Ngaruawahia
SOUTHERN END	Hamilton
DISTANCE	11 km
MAPS	35, 36
TRACK STANDARD	Easy tramping

THE ROUTE FOLLOWS a lovely riverside path out of Ngaruawahia with time to study the Turangawaewae marae and its waka across the river. It continues along the golf course boundary, then onto the shoulder of Great South Rd to pass the AFFCO freezing works, before returning to the riverbank along Te Awa, a joint Te Araroa and cycleway project. Fonterra has allowed access behind its Te Rapa milk-processing plant, and plans to open to public view a pa site there. The trail then crosses Equestrian Centre land, and Braithwaite Park.

After the confiscations of Maori land in 1865, steam haulers with glowing fireboxes crawled along the river-banks on rails laid upon imported willow sleepers. They bore away the kahikatea. That lowland forest vanished, and the imported sleepers sprouted and flourished. Farmers planted willow too, fast-growing grey willow and crack willow, and the river bore the silky catkins away. The Waikato River became edged with willow. It's gradually being cleared, and the final few kilometres into Hamilton are exemplary urban riverside. Residents have adopted the American habit of running their lawns or gardens seamlessly onto the public domain. The flower gardens, low rock walls and lawns are as open to the gaze of walkers as they are to the people who tend them, and the grassy banks of public land sloping to the river are similarly manicured. The river runs strong and open here, and Hamilton is a proud city.

...tly from the Hakarimata Track.

Conservation Volunteers team at work on the City to Mountain Trail.

JUST AFTER THE RAILWAY BRIDGE crosses the river, exit Te Awa up the Centennial Steps to Alma St. One block in from the river is Victoria St, Hamilton's main thoroughfare. Cross over, go through Garden Place and the Downtown Plaza Shopping Centre, and into Ward St. Two blocks up, Hamilton Girls' High School is on the left and Seddon Park, Hamilton's international cricket ground, is close by, north down Tristram St. Ward St leads left onto Tainui St and connects with Lake Domain Drive and a pleasant stroll 700 m along the shore of Lake Rotoroa. It's a shallow lake that Hamiltonians use for fishing, yachting and dragon-boat racing, and where you'll see ducks and perhaps the aerobatic swallow chasing down insect prey.

Exit onto Killarney Rd and follow it across the main trunk railway almost 2 km to the Dinsdale roundabout. Follow Whatawhata Rd another kilometre before turning up Melva St to Tills Lookout. The lookout rises to about 80 m, only 40 m or so above the surrounding country, but it's sufficient to glimpse, on a very clear day, the tip of Ruapehu's volcanic summit, 160 km south, as the crow flies.

HAMILTON CITY TRAVERSE

NORTHERN START	Bryce St
SOUTHERN END	Tills Lookout
DISTANCE	5 km
MAPS	36
TRACK STANDARD	Tramping

THE CONCRETE PATH that slopes away from Tills Lookout begins the 2.5 km track west to Taitua Arboretum's peaceful groves and lakes. Continue along Taitua Rd to the O'Dea Rd road-end and a track that leads across deer-farming and dairy land, then along back roads to Whatawhata. A petrol station and coffee house here offer food and drink.

Cross the State Highway 23 bridge and turn onto Te Pahu Rd. Ducking in behind the church, the track descends to the Waipa River, wide and smooth here, 30 km shy of Ngaruawahia, where it segues into the Waikato. The track stays beside the Waipa for almost 5 km, diverts to a Te Pahu Rd road bridge at one point, then returns to the riverside, through to Old Mountain Rd and an uphill walk for 5 km. Turn left onto DOC's 7.5 km Karamu Track. This is a popular tramp across high, rocky farmland on the Kapamahunga Range. The Waikato plains spread wide and green below, dwindling east to a distant Kaimai Range. Farm animals may wander across your path here, and ahead is the long and broken summit of Pirongia.

At the Karamu's southern track-end, turn right onto Limeworks Loop Rd and follow it to the Kaniwhaniwha car

CITY TO MOUNTAIN TRAIL

NORTHERN START	Tills Lookout, Hamilton
SOUTHERN END	Pirongia summit
DISTANCE	40 km
MAPS	36, 37, 38
TRACK STANDARD	Tramping

park. Kaniwhaniwha camp is a pleasant 2.5 km walk in, and has toilets and a swimming hole before the Tahuanui Track begins its climb to the Pirongia summit.

Pirongia (959 m) is the Waikato's highest mountain, an extinct shield volcano from a rift that, around two million years ago, threw up Karioi to the west and the smaller Kakepuku to the east. It remains a sombre pile with winter sleet and snowfall on the summit, and should be treated seriously. Its peaty surfaces turn easily to mud, and the 7 km climb to the summit is often steep and slippery. Watch for pahautea, New Zealand mountain cedar, on the way up. It's common further south, but close to its cold-climate limits here, and making a first appearance on Te Araroa. The dead trunks on the ridges are pahautea also, perished perhaps from old age, but maybe also victims of a warming climate.

You can get lucky at the summit platform with views that include the mountains of the Central Plateau and Mt Taranaki, or you may just get cloud. A further downhill kilometre leads to Pahautea Hut. It's the first DOC hut on Te Araroa's route so far, and there's hut learnings. The first in get the bunks — but there's also well-drained tent sites alongside. Be tidy and don't spread out your cooking or tramping gear until you're sure you're going to be alone. Clean the hut when you leave, and shut the door. Hut books are also important. Some trampers have fun with the hut book here — either that or we must believe Barack Obama, Osama bin Laden and Elvis Presley have preceded us onto this summit. But the hut book should be treated as a vital record of arrival and departure dates. Any SAR team that seeks to locate an overdue tramper needs accurate information, and you should fill in your own arrival and departure dates.

McColl, section-tramper, and farmer, Karamu Track.

with a view, Pirongia, City to Mountain Trail.

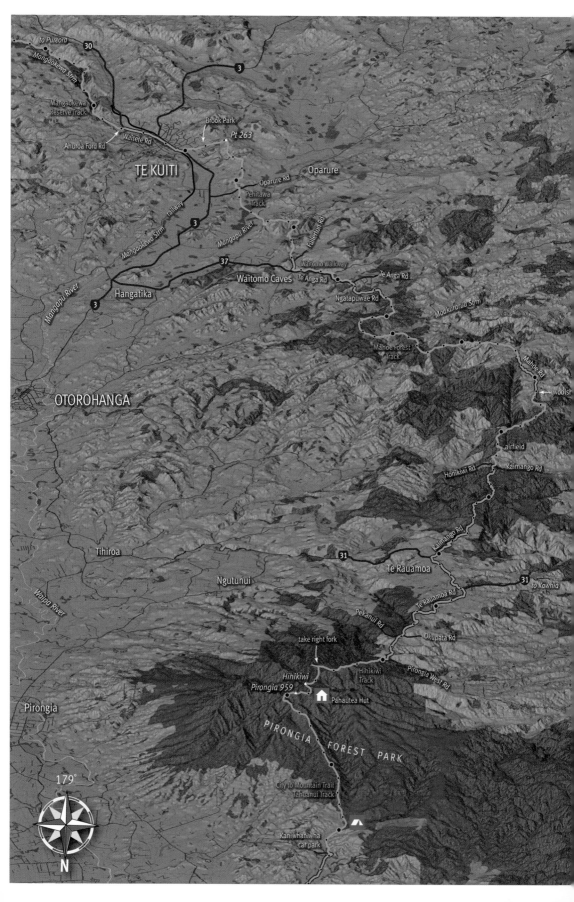

FROM PAHAUTEA HUT, continue southwest on the 800 m Noel Sandford boardwalk. Noel, TAT's construction manager, began building the boardwalk in 2005, on low budgets, in thick mud, over difficult grades, with a frequently clagged-in summit, and using school-pupil labour. Progress was slow until engineer Trevor Butler suggested using prefabricated sections, juggled to fit on site. Noel arranged Year 12 carpentry students at eight Waikato schools to build 120 sections and, in February 2007, supervised their placement on the mountaintop by RNZAF's No 3 Iroquois Squadron. Soon after, DOC got a budgetary allocation for the boardwalk and took over the finishing.

The boardwalk leads through to a lookout at Hihikiwi Peak, with views over the Aotea and Kawhia harbours on the west coast. Follow the track down to a spur where the Hihikiwi Track leads away to the right, down steep steps to Pirongia West Rd.

Follow Pirongia West Rd to its intersection with Pekanui Rd. Continue straight ahead along Te Rauamoa Rd to State Highway 31. Turn left on the highway and follow along to Kaimango Rd. Follow Kaimango Rd for 8.5 km to the intersection with Honikiwi Rd. Stay on Kaimango Rd for another 50 metres to a small car park where the road bends right.

HIHIKIWI TRACK

NORTHERN START	Pirongia summit
SOUTHERN END	Pirongia West Rd
DISTANCE	5.5 km
MAPS	38, 39
TRACK STANDARD	Tramping

FROM THE CAR PARK, cross the stile onto a farm road through to the airfield. Five hundred metres beyond it the track leaves the formed farm road for an old timber trail through to a woolshed at the Mahoe Rd road-end. Follow Mahoe Rd for a short while before taking a left, over a stile, and following the marked route mainly along fence line across a farm. On a good day there are great views across the King Country to the Central Plateau.

A short distance into the farm there is an airstrip, which can be a significant hazard when in use. Follow the instructions on the signs — waiting on the edge of the airstrip, gaining the attention of the site manager and only crossing when instructed.

After crossing the farm, the marked route will take you back into some very pleasant forest walking.

Follow along downhill to a crossing of Moakurarua Stream. This is a significant wade, and can be dangerous after persistent rain, so don't attempt this track in wet

MAHOE FOREST TRACK

NORTHERN START	Kaimango Rd car park
SOUTHERN END	Waitomo Village
DISTANCE	27 km
MAPS	39
TRACK STANDARD	Tramping

weather. Ngatapuwae Rd leads away south as a clay track that turns into a metalled road, joining to Te Anga Rd. At this intersection, look for orange markers 20 m to the right. The track leads down a steep bluff, and joins to DOC's Waitomo Walkway into Waitomo village.

Waitomo is famous for caves, glow worms and plump stalagmites. The Waitomo Caves Hotel, which sits on a promontory above it all as a somewhat faded Victorian and Art Deco marvel, occasionally reports, perhaps to balance such subterranean wonders, the supernatural thrill of a hotel ghost.

Walk east along Te Anga Rd and turn into Fullerton Rd. Follow it 1 km to a stile on the left-hand side.

PEHITAWA TRACK

NORTHERN START	Fullerton Rd
SOUTHERN END	Te Kuiti
DISTANCE	12.5 km
MAPS	39, 40
TRACK STANDARD	Tramping
NOTE	Closed for lambing August 1-September 30

FROM FULLERTON RD, follow orange markers across private farmland to the first of three steep, bush-covered hills. The ridgeline of the third hill has great views out over this tumbled karst landscape, then descends onto a farm race. Cross a farm bridge and look for a stile on the left and a swing bridge over the Mangapu River. The track then enters the tall, beautiful Pehitawa kahikatea forest, a protected remnant, and the best you'll see on Te Araroa.

The track climbs to cross Oparure Rd, and onto more private farmland. Just 50 m to the left of the track are two old trees with a great story attached of utu, shrewd politics, and maybe humour. In 1883 Maori chief Mahuki seized a government party surveying the route for the main trunk line. Mahuki was furious at Wilson Hursthouse's recent role in sacking the peaceful village of Parihaka. Far from help in hostile King Country territory, the surveyors peered from their prison shed to see Maori writing their names on pigs and slitting the pigs' throats. Then the door of the cell crashed open and there stood their rescuer, Te Kooti, himself a legendary rebel who was just then persuading the government to grant him an amnesty. Whitinui Joseph, a kinsman of Mahuki, celebrated the peaceful resolution of this kidnap by planting two trees, a British holly and a native pohutukawa, that grow here still.

The track heads south another 3 km to a 263 m trig above Te Kuiti. Then it's down and out through Brook Park, following the blue track to its exit on the northern outskirts of Te Kuiti.

Ngatapuwae Rd.

Mahoe Forest Track.

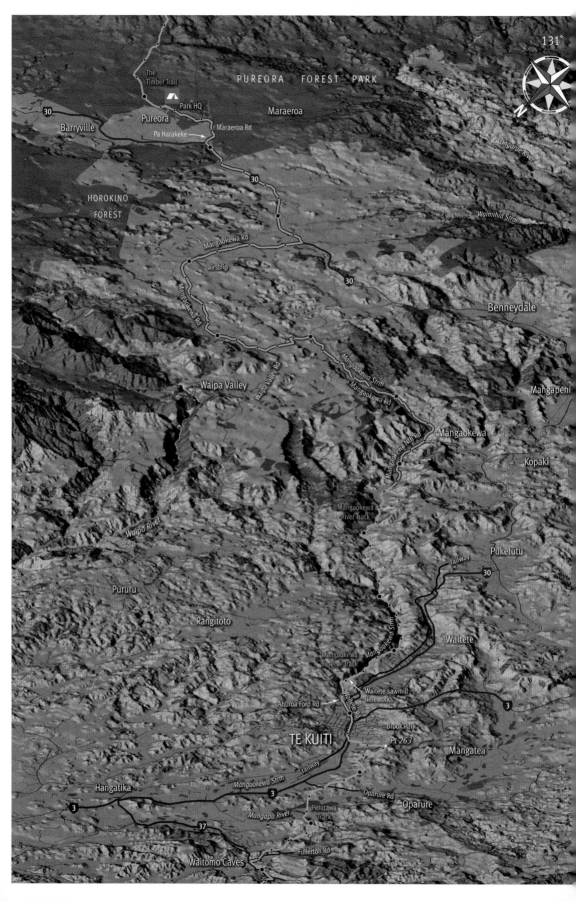

PUREORA   FOREST   PARK

Maraeroa

The Timber Trail

Park HQ

Pureora

Barryville

30

Pa Harakeke

Maraeroa Rd

Ongarue River

30

HOROKINO

FOREST

Waimihia Strm

Mangaokewa Rd

airstrip

30

Benneydale

Mangaokewa Rd

Waipa Valley

Waipa Valley Rd

Mangaokewa Strm

Mangaokewa Rd

Mangapehi

Mangaokewa

Kopaki

Mangaokewa Nth Rd

Waipa River

Mangaokewa
River Track

Pururu

Rangitoto

railway

Puketutu

30

Mangaokewa Strm

Waitete

Mangaokewa
Reserve Track

Waitete sawmill
limeworks

Ahuroa Ford Rd

Waitete Rd

3

TE KUITI

Brook Park
Pt 263

Mangatea

Hangatika

Mangaokewa Strm

railway

3

Oparure Rd

Oparure

3

Mangapu River

Pehitawa
Track

37

Fullerton Rd

Waitomo Caves

FROM THE SHEARING STATUE, continue south along Waitete Rd/State Highway 30 for just over 1 km, then turn left onto Ahuroa Ford Rd down to the Mangaokewa Stream. Turn right onto the riverbank and follow it without crossing the river. The track skirts Waitete Sawmills and McDonald's Limeworks, with a kiln producing burnt lime for roadworks as well as powdered lime for its many other uses, from toothpaste to top dressing. You'll also pass close to an old cement works, then cross the river on a vehicle bridge.

Once across the river, the track follows a disused quarry road to an abandoned lime quarry, with pipeline and wooden tower remnants. The track ascends beyond the quarry to an elevation of 100 m, with good views back across Te Kuiti township and up the valley ahead. Te Kuiti High School students built the picnic table at this viewpoint, and also, as you descend again towards the river, the footbridges across side creeks.

The track enters bush for the last kilometre, passing one pretty waterfall en route, then crosses the river into Mangaokewa Reserve on a suspension bridge.

MANGAOKEWA RESERVE TRACK

NORTHERN START	Te Kuiti
SOUTHERN END	Mangaokewa Reserve
DISTANCE	4.5 km
MAPS	40
TRACK STANDARD	Easy tramping

TRACKS LEAD AWAY on both sides of the river so stay on the true left bank — that is, the side you've just crossed onto to reach the reserve. The Mangaokewa River Track stays on this true left throughout.

The first 2.5 km of bush is lush and nearly predator free, thanks to the local Mangaokewa Reserve Trust, which has also released native birds here. You'll pass a huge kahikatea, and through the riverside bush may glimpse stalactites encrusting the far edge of this deeply incised limestone gorge.

The trail then crosses a fence put in to keep sheep out of the reserve and breaks into farmland. A swing bridge on the left crosses the river and is part of a loop track around the reserve. Te Araroa heads straight on, upstream.

Continuing on across farmland, you'll see primeval forest on the opposite side of the river — it's as good as a diorama of everything that's noble about an untouched New Zealand forest, and it's life size. The track stays on farmland, passes an abandoned dunny, glides through numerous totara glades and suggests great picnic spots on the way through. It enters the shade of pine and eucalypt forest near the southern end, where you pass a

MANGAOKEWA RIVER TRACK

NORTHERN START	Mangaokewa Reserve
SOUTHERN END	Mangaokewa North Rd
DISTANCE	15 km
MAPS	41, 42, 43
TRACK STANDARD	Tramping

gate leading to a farm track with a grass median strip. This track leads through to Mangaokewa North Rd road-end. There's no camping or accommodation at Mangaokewa North Rd and if tramping this track one way, you'll need to arrange a reliable pick-up — it's a long way from anywhere and there's no passing traffic to hitchhike out with.

Through-walkers follow Mangaokewa North Rd out to the road junction. Turn left onto Mangaokewa Rd and stay on this road for 26 km through to State Highway 30. Turn left down the highway and 8.5 km along, Maraeroa Rd leads away to the right, connecting via Barryville then Village roads to Pureora Forest Park Headquarters.

The Headquarters has a basic campsite and cabins with kitchen facilities, but these should be booked ahead.

There are no retail facilities at Pureora, though you can buy coffee and a snack from Pa Harakeke on Maraeroa Rd. The roadwalk from Mangaokewa River to Pureora is a long one and TAT is working to reduce it.

Te Kuiti Rotary's Ray Scrimgeour cuts grass on the Mangaokewa Reserve Track.

Ian Pryce, section-tramper, Mangaokewa Track.

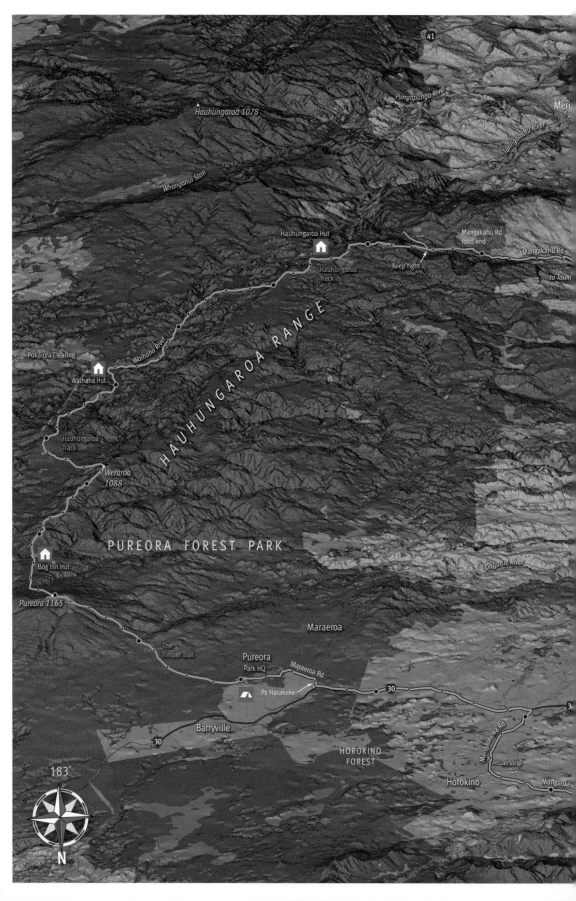

TE ARAROA FOLLOWS the south-bound Timber Trail for the first 8 km out of Pureora field centre, then branches away left to the Mt Pureora summit (1165 m). Together with its nearby twin, Titiraupenga, Pureora is an old volcano standing clear of the surrounding forest, and it overlooks New Zealand's most fearsome terrain.

To the south, the distant Ruapehu and Ngauruhoe volcanoes are intermittently active but these mountains are respected more than feared. The calderas are different. You can see eight from your Pureora perch. Taupo, to the northeast, is most easily recognised because the huge collapsed crater is now a glassy lake. As you swing your gaze around from there, the other calderas are less distinct, part and parcel of the grotesque contours that droop away north.

In prehistory, Taupo blew out an unimaginably vast 1000 cubic kilometres of material. More recently, in 233 AD, it blew out another 100 cubic kilometres — a smaller eruption, but the biggest since humanity's written records began. Chinese and Roman scribes recorded red crepuscular skies. If you did the Buried Forest walk back at Pureora village, you'll know already that this eruption's shock wave knocked down a forest and covered it deep in pumice and ash.

All the calderas remain potentially explosive, but the geological sequence of their eruptions is so long that Kiwis have grown blithe. Occasionally, though, geological time is now: the distant Okataina caldera includes Tarawera, the slug of docile land that in 1886 split into seven roaring volcanic throats, overwhelming nearby Maori villages and the once-famous Pink and White Terraces.

The track heads south off Pureora 3.5 km to Bog Inn, on the margin of a mountain mire. On the next 18 km leg through to Waihaha Hut the track goes over two prominent summits with glimpses down onto Lake Taupo. You may get birdsong — the native pigeon kereru's low note; the onomatopoeic kaka, the bush parrot; kakariki, the bush parakeet; and the pitoitoi, the small robin likely to hop around at ground level, always attentive. Some trampers have reported kokako, the bird with the blue wattles, the black eye-mask and the glassy gonging voice, but it's rare.

Back at the Pureora Forest Park Headquarters you may also have done the Totara Walk. Those forest giants were saved by a tree-top protest in 1978, when a group of 12 climbed the big podocarps, set up platforms and leg-roped themselves into place. New Zealand Forest Service loggers

HAUHUNGAROA TRACK

NORTHERN START	DOC Pureora village
SOUTHERN END	Waituhi Rd
DISTANCE	54 km
MAPS	43, 44, 45
TRACK STANDARD	Tramping

thought they were bluffing, but as they felled one of the big totara, a protester just 10 m away called down from the tops. The shocked foresters downed tools, and Pureora's podocarps were never again felled. A protest leader at that time, Stephen King, called this antique forest 'the old mansion', and you'll see certain pillars of it as you drop down towards Waihaha Hut for a second stopover.

Following along inland from the hut, look for the native duck, the whio. Comparatively rare, they ride the Waihaha River around here, a very distinct and confident duck that likes white water. Thirteen kilometres on, the Hauhungaroa Hut is sited at 950 m with good views out to the northwest. It's new and, like all the huts, has a wood stove.

Four and a half kilometres past Hauhungaroa Hut, there's a turnoff to the left, but keep going straight ahead another 2 km to the end of Mangakahu Road. Be aware you are then still a considerable distance from civilisation, and if doing a through-walk will need to allow a further day's walk to gain Taumarunui, the resupply township.

Walk out to Taumarunui via Mangakahu, Ongarue and Taumarunui-Ngapuke Rd, then Golf Road and Short Street. This is a 35 km roadwalk.

From Taumarunui, walk State Highway 4 south to Owhango Village. This is another 20 km roadwalk.

Resting up at Hauhungaroa Hut.

Mt Pureroa summit (foreground), Mt Pureroa Forest Park.

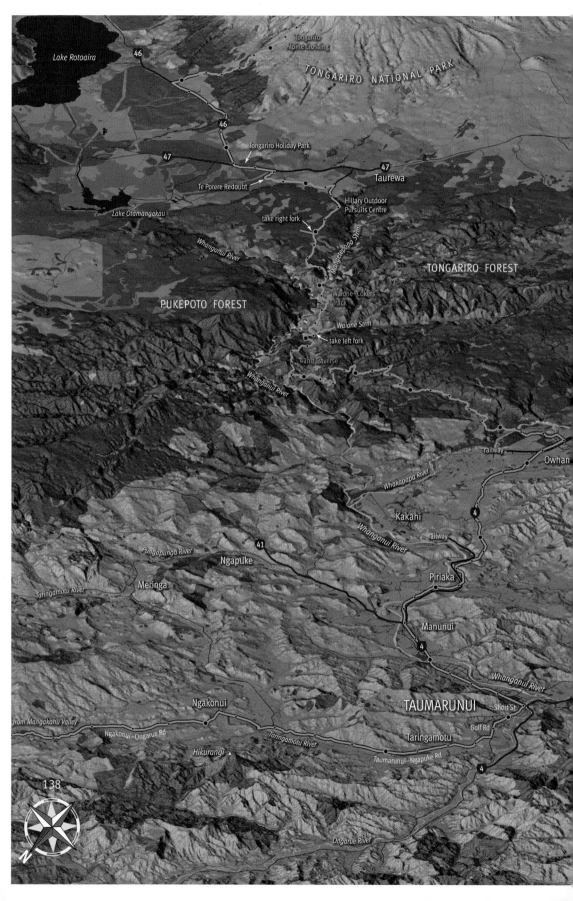

Lake Rotoaira

46

Tongariro
Alpine Crossing

TONGARIRO NATIONAL PARK

46

47

Tongariro Holiday Park

47

Taurewa

Te Porere Redoubt

Hillary Outdoor
Pursuits Centre

take right fork

TONGARIRO FOREST

Lake Otamangakau

Whanganui River

Mangatepopo Strm

PUKEPOTO FOREST

Waione–Cokers
Track

Waione Strm

take left fork

Whanganui River

42nd Traverse

railway

Owhan

Whakapapa River

Kakahi

4

Whanganui River

railway

41

Pungapunga River

Ngapuke

Piriaka

Meringa

Taringamotu River

Manunui

4

Whanganui River

TAUMARUNUI

Short St

Ngakonui

from Mangakahu Valley

Ngakonui–Ongarue Rd

Taringamotu River

Golf Rd

Taringamotu

Taumarunui–Ngapuke Rd

4

Hikurangi

Ongarue River

N

TE ARAROA STEPS AWAY from the 42 Traverse after the first 24 km, but for that first part, trampers will be treading a multi-use track. From December 1 to April 30 each year the 42 Traverse is open to motorcyclists and four-wheel-drives, and is also a favourite mountain-bike route, generally biked from south to north. If you're tramping in summer, therefore, be prepared to occasionally step aside.

The track rises only 400 m in a 39 km traverse, but it crosses crinkled terrain, with many descents into gullies, including two deeper watercourses, the Waione Stream and the Mangatepopo Stream. The flat plateau of Tongariro and the scoria cone of Ngauruhoe form a distant grey tableau beyond a lush green montane forest cover. The forest was once heavily logged, but is tagged as a 'future forest' after being saved as part of New Zealand's Public Conservation Land in the late 1980s. It's rich in berries, there's birdsong everywhere, and it's a kiwi sanctuary with no dogs permitted. You walk forest roads put in by D8 bulldozers, so they're well benched and the deep cuttings reveal successive layers of pumice and grit from the Taupo eruptions and other volcanic events.

Twenty-four kilometres in, you cross the Waione Stream and leave the 42 Traverse for the Waione–Cokers Track. The only vehicles that now use this track are quad bikes that service the pest-baiting stations. Four kilometres in from the turnoff a steep pumice slope takes you down to the Mangatepopo Stream rapids. Head upstream on a small side braid, and at the top of the rapids you'll see a track opposite where some quads apparently make landfall, but it's still not a good cross point. Another 20 m upstream the river shoals slightly and here, provided there's been no recent heavy rain, it's an easy wade across.

A clay track climbs steeply away from the Mangatepopo, levelling out at 600 m with wide views down onto the Whanganui River and the substantial peaks of Kakaramea (1300 m) and Pihanga (1325 m) rising behind. What will later be a great river is shallow and boulder-strewn here, just 20 km from its source on Tongariro.

The trail then bears right at the only substantial intersection, to finish opposite the Hillary Outdoor Pursuits Centre, New Zealand's leading outdoor adventure centre for school students and corporate teams. A short road section leads to a turnoff that tracks through to

MODIFIED 42 TRAVERSE

NORTHERN START	Owhango
SOUTHERN END	Tongariro Holiday Park
DISTANCE	39 km
MAPS	48, 49, 50
TRACK STANDARD	Tramping

first the upper, then the lower Te Porere Redoubt. These earthen defensive works have been restored and are in good condition — relics of a turning point in the violent history of the Maori leader Te Kooti.

Originally imprisoned on the Chatham Islands, Te Kooti had escaped in 1868 with 300 followers. After coming ashore at Poverty Bay he began a reign of terror with the ruthless killing of 54 people at Matawhero on the outskirts of Gisborne. Te Kooti began a personal war, but the recent withdrawal of imperial troops from New Zealand, and the easily combustible grievances of the recent Waikato and Taranaki wars lent his campaign an extra dimension of terror.

The campaign to stop him was urgent. He was hunted to Te Porere and colonial troops and kupapa warriors (Maori fighting for the British) from Whanganui frontally attacked and overran these redoubts. Though a brilliant guerrilla tactician, Te Kooti had not mastered pa construction. The defensive ditches weren't deep enough, the redoubts weren't built for enfilade fire, and their loopholes didn't allow sufficient angle of fire downwards. It should have been a final victory, but a sketch of the battle, drawn at the time and reproduced on the notice board here, shows, along with the sweeping arrows of the successful rout, one poignant addition — the stick figure of Te Kooti escaping out the back.

The guerrilla leader fled into the King Country and remained elusive, but without significant victories his power diminished. He was pardoned in 1883, as part of the Maori King's reconciliation with the colonial government, but as founder of the Ringatu religion continued to lead a band of followers, and remained a figure of dread in Poverty Bay.

From Te Porere it's a 1.5 km road-walk through to the Tongariro Holiday Park.

Walk around on State Highways 47 and 46 to the start of the Tongariro Crossing.

uruhoe from the 42 Traverse.

npers crossing Mangatepopo Stream, 42 Traverse.

whanganui and manawatu

whanganui

THE LAND

As you cross their mountain flanks, Tongariro, Ngauruhoe, and Ruapehu will show you the glassy pleasures of altitude. Blue sky, maybe the last traces of snow, and a charming volcanic quietude — nothing more than a whiff of sulphurous gas here, a small blast of steam there, or bright colours in the lakes. It's a heady mix, and Te Araroa's route across the Central Plateau samples all of it.

The land to the west is soft papa country. Rivers slice it like butter and backblocks farmers live with the rumble of its landslides. The Whanganui River winds through it in a deep cleft, but not gorgey at all, just fern-hung and pretty. Te Araroa canoes a long section of this river.

Papa is a siltstone, product of an undersea sedimentary basin that's been gently uplifted, and the Whanganui's banks are often distinctly layered and speckled with fossil shells. Uplift of an undersea sedimentary basin as young as this one is unusual. The preservation of the basin's fossil shells in regular and separate sequences, interspersed with easily dateable eruption layers from the nearby volcanoes, is also unusual. The shellfish species differ nicely too in response to long-ago changes in ocean temperatures and sea levels. Warm or cold, high or low, the bands of shell remnants are an accurate map of temperature change over millions of years, and Whanganui's layered papa is one of the world's best records of change in climatic patterns. If there's a person standing in front of any cliff or bank as you pass through Whanganui and stroking their chin, it's likely to be a palaeoclimatologist.

THE PEOPLE

Ngati Tuwharetoa's paramount chief, Horonuku, signed over the summits of the three mountains to the Crown in 1887 and this great gift became the nucleus of the North Island's most accessible wilderness park. Maori myth unifies the main mountains — a tale of lovers in an impossible threesome, the loser gouging the channel of the Whanganui River as he retreated to the coast. It's a good story, evocative of mood and mana, and of painful choices between love and loyalty. The mountain woman is sometimes said to be Pihanga, and sometimes Ruapehu, but if ever the woman of the story looks west to the now-distant and perfect form of Taranaki and sighs for her lost love, then the sighing woman is always Ruapehu.

Indeed she sighs. The mountain regularly erupts steam and ash, lava rarely, and lahars sometimes. On Christmas Eve 1953 as the overnight express train to Auckland sped through the night, a lahar from Ruapehu's distant summit demolished the bridge in front of the train, and 151 people died.

Provincial Whanganui rears mainly sheep and cattle, and though the back country is notoriously hard, the land around Whanganui city is famously fertile, flat and prosperously farmed. The city at the river mouth is one of New Zealand's oldest and smallest and most remote, and something about that combination has kept the wrecker's ball at bay. Whanganui's early European buildings remain picturesquely in place on the main streets and in the parks, and the city is attentive to its past, with citizen groups resurrecting its coal-fired river steamers, and a tram.

manawatu

THE LAND

The rivers bring sand-sized sediments down to the coast, longshore drift brings in further sediments from the sea, and the westerlies here are strong enough to blow it all back inland. The winds build sand dunes on the coast, but over time the dunes have moved inland too, for tens of kilometres. The further in, the older they get, until finally they're simply a stable and hummocky part of this low landscape. The dunes blow in from the west and meet the plains of alluvium carried down from the ranges in the east — that, in short, is the Manawatu Plains.

It takes big rivers to build alluvial plains, and Te Araroa crosses the first of them, the Rangitikei, at Bulls, then heads towards a crossing of the Manawatu River, at Palmerston North. The river looks slow and steady at Palmerston North but the stopbanks either side hint at its power, and just 22 km upstream it's done what no other river in New Zealand has even come close to doing: sawn right through a mountain range. The celebrated Manawatu Gorge water gap is the result of an abrasive river eroding its way through a mountain range faster than the range is rising.

Water gaps are also wind gaps. New Zealand's first big wind farms were built here, 400 m up, their long blades churning above the clouds like marathon swimmers heading determinedly along the range. Te Araroa will do the same but on foot and gaining more ground. Beyond Palmerston North it heads into the Tararua foothills on a track that exits close to Levin.

THE PEOPLE

In 1864, Rangitane chief Te Peeti Awe Awe sold the government a large block of land running parallel to the Ruahine and Tararua ranges. Government surveyors laid out Palmerston North at the southern end of the block, with long, straight roads and a generous 7 hectares of open space where the two main roads crossed. That's now a large town square, and Te Peeti's dying words of 1884 are inscribed here: *Kua kaupapa i au te aroha ma koutou e whakaoti* — I have laid the foundation of love for you to build upon.

Te Peeti's Rangitane warriors joined with Te Keepa's Whanganui warriors to fight alongside the Crown in the 1860s. He believed in the new city, and the city remembers.

Palmerston North is the urban heart of the Manawatu, largeish, but not so large that it forgets its founding families. They came from Britain and some from Scandinavia. They beat back forest and swamp. They drove the railroads through and when all that was done they set to work farming: dairy, sheep and cattle. The city continues in that tough pastoral tradition as an open, inclusive place enlivened now by a stimulating library, by the only professional live theatre outside of New Zealand's big four cities, and by the mutual town-and-gown stimulus of having Massey University across the river.

Te Araroa passes also through Feilding, an English settler town only slightly younger than its nearby city and hewn, as Palmerston North was, from forest and swamp. On Fridays if you time your walk right, the country comes to town with a famously vigorous stockyard sale.

Mt Ruapehu on the Central Plateau.

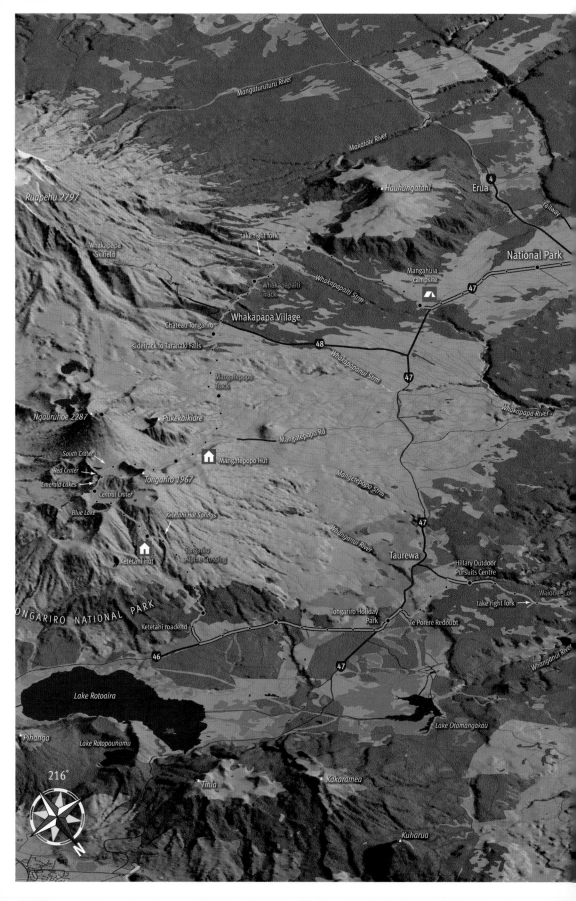

THE TONGARIRO ALPINE CROSSING is New Zealand's most famous one-day tramp. It can also be dangerous, so before starting out, it's a sensible precaution to ring DOC's Ruapehu Area Office for a weather update.

The track heads out through podocarp forest, runs alongside a mineral-rich stream for a time, crosses over an old lava tongue, then breaks out of the forest onto tussock. Ahead, and high above, the steam from Ketetahi Springs is a wafting flag, and it's nearly 3 km of uphill grunt before you get past this hissing and sulphurous cleft to reach Ketetahi Shelter.

From the hut deck, the landscape below is spread out wide and clean, the circular Lake Rotoaira at your feet, the volcanic shoulders of Kakaramea and Pihanga hunched above it, and beyond them, Taupo's polished surface stretching to the northern horizon.

The track then zigzags rapidly to gain another 300 m of altitude and breaks out onto Tongariro's flat Central Crater at 1700 m. Tongariro is the oldest of the Central Plateau's volcanic mountains and as if to compensate for the ravages of great age is hung with a kind of jewellery — the Blue and Emerald Lakes, and the flat round cameos of ancient craters. A slog up loose scoria to the top of Red Crater takes you to 1868 m and the highest point on the Crossing, with an outlook across the mountain's great lava buttresses to the Kaimanawa Range in the east, and the Rangipo Desert in the south. The side trip to Tongariro's summit (1967 m) from here is a one-and-a-half hour return tramp.

From Red Crater the track descends on a steep poled route into South Crater. This crater is also flat, but Ngauruhoe's symmetrical cone rises alongside, and if you find that irresistible, it's a three-hour return climb to the summit, a simple side trip if you're fit.

Continuing on, the track leaves South Crater on a steep descent into the Mangatepopo Valley and onward from there across a tidily boardwalked and nicely maintained track to Mangetepopo Hut.

Through-walkers take the turnoff left, just past the hut. Day-walkers may wish to continue on to what is the usual southern start point of the Tongariro Alpine Crossing, and which here, since the track has been walked on a less usual north-to-south traverse, becomes an end point — the Mangatepopo road-end.

TONGARIRO ALPINE CROSSING

NORTHERN START	Ketetahi Rd road-end, off State Highway 46
SOUTHERN END	Mangatepopo Hut
DISTANCE	18 km
MAPS	50
TRACK STANDARD	Tramping

MANGATEPOPO TRACK

NORTHERN START	Mangatepopo Hut
SOUTHERN END	Whakapapa Village
DISTANCE	9.5 km
MAPS	51
TRACK STANDARD	Tramping

JUST BEYOND THE MANGATEPOPO HUT, the Mangatepopo Track, often referred to as the Ditch Track, turns left towards Ruapehu. The first 3 km skirts around Pukekaikiore on Ngauruhoe's western flank, then moves across tussock and shrubland at the foot of Ruapehu.

Streams that drain both Ngauruhoe and Ruapehu have scoured the ash and debris of the slopes, and though the major streams on this track are bridged, the approaches to bridged and unbridged watercourses alike are often washed out — ditch by name and ditch by nature.

Part-way along this route the Chateau Tongariro appears in the distance as a somewhat unlikely four-storey apparition, magnificent and alone. The Georgian-style hotel was built in 1929 by a private tourism company to begin what was billed as an era of elegant tourism. The elegance was somewhat interrupted by the Depression and World War II, and the New Zealand government took over the Chateau in 1957, then on-sold it in 1990. Throughout that history, the Chateau's old-world charm has endeared it to generations of Kiwis.

For the last 2 km the track enters beech forest, then joins the Lower Taranaki Falls Track to emerge at Whakapapa Village. The mountain village has a motor camp, a store and accommodation options.

WHAKAPAPAITI TRACK

NORTHERN START	Whakapapa Village
SOUTHERN END	Mangahuia Camp
DISTANCE	12 km
MAPS	51
TRACK STANDARD	Tramping

THE TRACK STARTS opposite the Whakapapa Village Fire Station, and crosses one of Ruapehu's bigger streams, the Whakapapanui, on a footbridge. It's walking standard as it heads out, undulating pleasantly through beech forest with groves of kaiwaka and cabbage trees. All but the shallowest streams are bridged.

Immediately after the fifth bridge, across the Whakapapaiti Stream, there's a junction. Turn right and descend through tussock and occasional boggy patches to the Mangahuia Camp where there's a car park, a picnic area and toilets.

Walk through on State Highway 45 to the National Park settlement. The service station has a well-stocked shop, and the settlement has a range of accommodation, from luxury to backpacker.

uruhoe and Red Crater, Tongariro Alpine Crossing.

tral Crater, Tongariro Alpine Crossing.

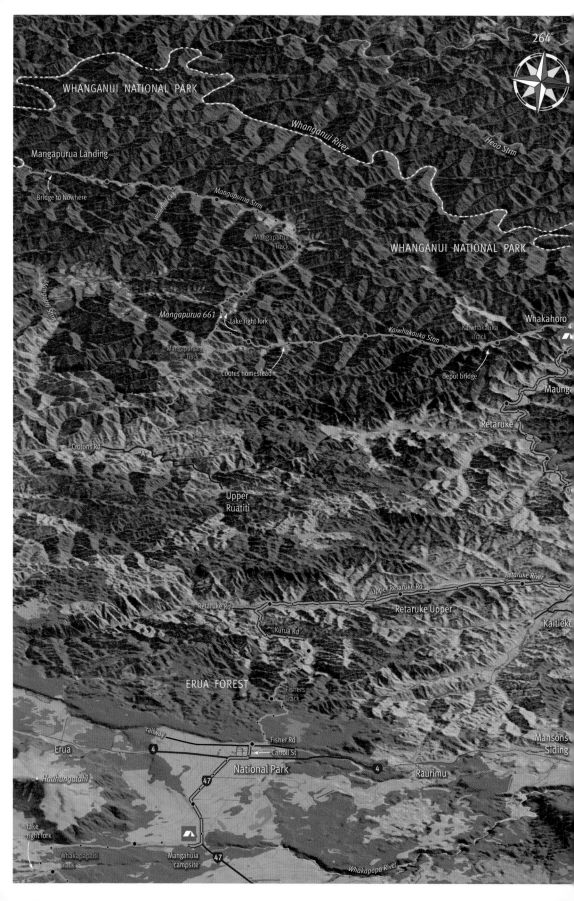

264°

WHANGANUI NATIONAL PARK

Whanganui River

Heao Strm

Mangapurua Landing

Bridge to Nowhere

Waterfall Ck

Mangapurua Strm

Mangapurua Strm

Mangapurua Track

WHANGANUI NATIONAL PARK

Whakahoro

Mangapurua 661

take right fork

Kaiwhakauka Strm

Kaiwhakauka Track

Mangapurua Track

Cootes homestead

depot bridge

Maung

Crotons Rd

"A"

Retaruke

Upper
Ruatiti

Retaruke River

Upper Retaruke Rd

Retaruke Rd

Retaruke Upper

Kaitieke

Kurua Rd

Oi

ERUA FOREST

Fishers Track

railway

Mansons
Siding

Erua

4

Fisher Rd

Carroll St

Hauhungatahi

National Park

4

Raurimu

47

take
right fork

Whakapapaiti Track

Mangahuia campsite

47

Whakapapa River

FISHERS TRACK

NORTHERN START	National Park
SOUTHERN END	Retaruke Rd
DISTANCE	15 km
MAPS	52, 53
TRACK STANDARD	Tramping

CROSS THE RAILWAY LINE on Carroll St, National Park, and turn left onto Fisher Rd, a surveyed and benched road, passable now only to mountain bikers and trampers. For the first kilometre it's a metalled road. As you crest the first ridge at 800 m and enter Erua Forest, though, toitoi drapes across the narrowing clay thoroughfare. The track heads along a flat ridge for 4 km, and in glimpses through low forest you'll occasionally spot Mt Taranaki's near-perfect peak 110 km to the west. The track then comes up to an intersection with an apparently more substantial route heading away right. Fishers Track bears left here, then drops steeply away for 1 km into farming country. Here the track is grassed, though occasionally boggy from farm use. It's now 5 km out to Kurua Rd, a little-used back road that connects through to Retaruke Rd.

Walk up Retaruke Rd and turn left at the war memorial into Oio Rd through to Whakahoro Camp.

KAIWHAKAUKA TRACK

NORTHERN START	Whakahoro
SOUTHERN END	Mangapurua Track junction
DISTANCE	16 km
MAPS	54
TRACK STANDARD	Tramping

AN OLD ROAD leads away from the camp and turns inland to follow the Kaiwhakauka Stream 4 km to reach the Depot Bridge. The old truss bridge dates from the 1920s, when farming ambitions in this valley were high, but a swing bridge now takes walkers across to the Kaiwhakauka's true left bank. The route onward through open river flats and lowland forest canopies is easy, with most of the side streams bridged, so it's a route also often used by mountain bikers.

Eleven kilometres along you'll sight the chimney stack of the old Cootes homestead. This solitary brick finger is part of a farming story that begins in this valley and unrolls more fully as you turn right at the head of the Kaiwhakauka Valley and head down the long Mangapurua Valley. It's the story of a pioneering farming enterprise, and the final poignant symbol of its failure — the Bridge to Nowhere.

MANGAPURUA TRACK

NORTHERN START	Kaiwhakauka Track junction
SOUTHERN END	Mangapurua Landing
DISTANCE	21 km
MAPS	54, 55, 56
TRACK STANDARD	Tramping

NEW ZEALAND SOLDIERS returning from World War I were young, fit and, after four years fighting overseas, adrift without occupation. The government offered them low-interest rehab loans together with newly surveyed back-country farming blocks. Rehab soldiers bought blocks in the remote Mangapurua Valley and with government help built the first hand-cranked cage crossings of the sheer-sided Mangapurua Stream, then swing bridges. They burned back the bush and sowed clover and canola and turnip seed in the ashes.

Over the tough but optimistic first years a strong valley community emerged with scratch sports teams, regular picnics at Waterfall Creek, and a school. Then, as the 1920s settled in, wool prices dropped from a post-war high of 12 cents a pound to 5 cents, and hard-nosed rural supply firms took much of the farmers' diminishing returns. Hunting and labouring payments that at first had merely supplemented farming income began to be a mainstay — a 5 cent bounty on pig snouts, and 80 cents a day for clearing the slips and mudslides from the government roads. The sunrise project turned gradually to something close to subsistence, and one by one they left. The farms broke hearts, and the last of the settlers pulled out in 1942.

As you turn off the Kaiwhakauka Track, climb for 1 km to the Mangapurua trig (661 m) with views through to Mt Taranaki in the west. It's then an easy walk on the old Mangapurua Rd gently downhill past the old poplar rows, pines, hand-split fence posts, pit-sawn planks and remnant chimneys of nine abandoned farms, through to the Bridge to Nowhere. The Ministry of Works built the bridge in 1936 to ease the hardships here, but it proved no more than the last rising of the flame on a doomed experiment.

Mangapurua Landing has no exit except a canoe paddle downriver, and your canoe delivery to the landing needs to be pre-booked. Jet boats can bring it in. They run regular trips in summer to service mountain bikers who use the Mangapurua Track. If no jet boat is running, however, then Te Araroa's Whanganui River section should start from Whakahoro, where the canoes or kayaks are more easily delivered.

ge to Nowhere, Mangapurua Track.

ding downstream from John Coull Hut towards the Bridge to Nowhere, Whanganui River.

YOU'RE NOW ON THE upper reaches of a very long, and very navigable, river. Maori coming upstream in their waka described its character here as matapihi — a window that opened upon the interior of Te Ika a Maui (the North Island). Upstream it took you towards volcanoes whose intermittent eruptions were seen as an omen of war. Here also, trails branched away to all parts of the island. Powerful iwi and their sub-tribes rubbed together, and quarrels often turned deadly. Pa stood on the cliffs with retractable vine ladders and boulders to roll or muskets to fire at hostile waka, and passage was often barred by an aukati — in 1856, missionaries reported a supplejack hung with bells near Mangapurua, a warning that any who passed that jangling line across the river could be killed. Even after the last of the guerilla campaigns had subsided in the 1880s, the Whanganui chief Te Keepa Te Rangihiwinui, a kupapa general and the Crown's greatest Maori hero, nonetheless placed an aukati at Mangapurua to stop any surveyor, government agent or potential buyer of Maori land from going upriver.

The first overnight camp is Tieke marae, 10.5 km downriver, with 20 bunks and a campsite. If you stop here, wait first at the shoreline. If no one comes to greet you, then go up and make yourself at home. Just across the river from here is the Ramanui campsite, within walking distance of the bar at the nearby Bridge to Nowhere Lodge.

The next potential stopping point is Ngaporo Camp, another 12.5 km downriver. Beyond it are two fairly benign rapids, before a look back at a scene that first appeared in the daguerreotypes of an earlier age: a Whanganui tableau, the so-called Drop Scene of perpendicular papa cliffs and a reflective river snaking away to vanish at the foot of a high, triangular bluff. Then it's the Puraroto Caves and a further 6 km paddle through two last rapids to the boat ramp at Pipiriki.

Pipiriki is the end point for most of the Whanganui canoe-hire companies, and to kayak on from here you'll need a further deal with the companies listed on TAT's website. Other options are walking the Whanganui River Rd, a two- or three-day tramp, or cycling it, which can be done in a day. See TAT website for accommodation options.

Jerusalem is an easy 11 km paddle further downriver. On approach, you'll spot the steeple of the Catholic church and discover the Whanganui is also a religious river. In the 1850s the Anglican Church Missionary Society's Richard Taylor and his Catholic rival Father Jean Lampila struggled

WHANGANUI RIVER (STAGE 1)

NORTHERN START	Mangapurua Landing
SOUTHERN END	Jerusalem
DISTANCE	41 km
MAPS	56, 57
TRACK STANDARD	River

for souls along the river's length. The Catholic father used the simple lure of flour mills, and once challenged Taylor to walk through fire. His Protestant opponent declined, but the Catholic did walk through the flames, and Maori around here loved it. Jerusalem, though named by Taylor, went Catholic.

Sister Suzanne Aubert arrived in 1883, to a place she claimed to have already seen in a dream. Amidst such mystical déjà vu she was distinctive also for the flash of a red flannel underskirt as she moved swiftly about. The slightly cross-eyed French nun learned te reo, cured ailments, set bones, ran a distillery to produce Maori medicine, marketed these indigenous salves and potions, planted cherry, walnut and chestnut trees, and sold the produce to steamboat river travellers. Within nine years she'd also founded the only new Catholic order in this country, the Sisters of Compassion, and written its constitution: 'The Sisters have been instituted solely for the Maori and the poor . . .' Sister Aubert is the closest New Zealand has had to a Catholic saint.

A short distance up from the convent, you can follow along where pilgrim feet have polished the tree roots, to a chiselled river stone that names 'Hemi — James Keir Baxter, i whanau 1928, i mate 1972'. Jim Baxter was one of the great New Zealand poets. In 1968 he began the labour here, as he wrote to a friend, of 'washing and cleaning' a side of the New Zealand spirit he felt was 'mangled and hurt' — the Maori side.

Ward, through-tramper, Whanganui River.

usalem, Whanganui River.

IMMEDIATELY BEYOND JERUSALEM there's another rapid, and 5 km further on a shingle island slightly wider and about four times longer than a rugby field. Apparently nondescript, it is a field of honour marked in Whanganui city, 75 km distant, with an elegant statue of white marble. This is Moutoa Island.

In the nineteenth century, Whanganui township was always in fear of what might burst upon it from upriver, and with good reason. In May 1864 waka taua from the interior stopped at Pipiriki for a swirling ceremony, and chants of 'Pai Marire — Hau! Hau! Hau!' around a newly erected rongo niu mast were heard. A new pan-tribal movement had arrived — millenarian, religious, prophetic, its warriors immune from bullets and more simply known as Hauhau. They were on a mission to drive Pakeha into the sea.

The war party sought passage from lower-river tribal leaders but was refused. The itinerant Hauhau — warriors, women, and children — then took over the village of Tawhitinui beside Moutoa Island and fortified it. Lower-river warriors gathered at Ranana, a settlement on the opposite bank. A purely Maori affair of mana was shaping up as a battle.

In the early morning of May 14 1864 over 100 Hauhau crossed to the upper end of Moutoa. Fifty lower-river defenders took up position in scrub at the middle of the island, with a further 50 reinforcements behind. For two hours the two sides exchanged challenges before the Hauhau danced a final peruperu, and charged. On the Tawhitinui river terraces, Hauhau women and children chanted the Pai Marire rites of protection. On the Ranana side, lower-river whanau called support to their fighters.

The thunder of shotguns. Gun smoke and confusion. The silence of the tomahawk, and the final despatch of the Hauhau leader by the patu paraoa. The battle lasted just half an hour. Fifty Hauhau were killed on the island or in retreat back across the river. The lower-river tribes lost 15, and Whanganui's citizens would erect a statue at Moutoa Gardens within the town's precincts to honour these fallen guardians. The fight by lower-river warriors had been for the mana of their river first of all, but the town fell under their protection too, and Whanganui was grateful.

At Ranana, just beyond Moutoa Island, there's hot showers and toilets, though any stay here should be booked in advance. The Kawana Mill, provided to river Maori by Governor George Grey in 1854, is another 5 km

WHANGANUI RIVER (STAGE 2)

NORTHERN START	Jerusalem
SOUTHERN END	Whanganui
DISTANCE	78 km
MAPS	57, 58, 59, 60
TRACK STANDARD	River

on and worth a stop. It's not well signposted from the river but the clue is a line of Lombardy poplars.

Koroniti marae on the true left bank further downriver, and the nearby cage-crossing of the river that marks the Flying Fox retreat, are both possible stops, but have to be booked ahead. Te Araroa trampers looking for good cheap passage can paddle on to DOC's one-ticket Downes Hut, a long day — 30 km altogether from Jerusalem — but doable.

Pungarehu, 17 km on from Downes, is a haul-out area for kayaks, but is 18 km short of Whanganui by road. If you keep going 11 km downriver, Hipango Park provides a camp and barbecue area. You're now within the tidal reaches of the river. It's wider and progressively harder to paddle, even more so with a headwind, and if you go on to Upokongaro 12 km distant, or Whanganui itself, you should time your run for an outgoing tide.

On the way into the city, you may see a plume of black coal smoke, and pushing around the bend the stately

Paddle steamer *Waimarie* on the Whanganui River.

paddle steamer *Waimarie*. The last great historical story of the Whanganui is the Victoran riverboat enterprise of Alexander Hatrick, whose paddle steamers plied a regular service to Pipiriki from 1892. By 1903, using shallow-draught boats with winches at the bow for haulage across rapids, and tunnel housings at the stern to protect the propellers, he'd expanded his passenger and farm supply service onward from Pipiriki to Taumarunui.

The Whanganui became, in this early period, a great tourist destination billed as the Rhine of New Zealand, with a grand hotel at Pipiriki, and well-appointed houseboat stopovers. Then the service turned from magnificent to quaint, to derelict, revived only recently with the restoration by volunteers of the *Waimarie* and the tunnel boat *Wairua*.

Walk out of Whanganui 20 km on State Highway 3. Turn right down Turakina Beach Rd to reach Koitiata settlement on the coast.

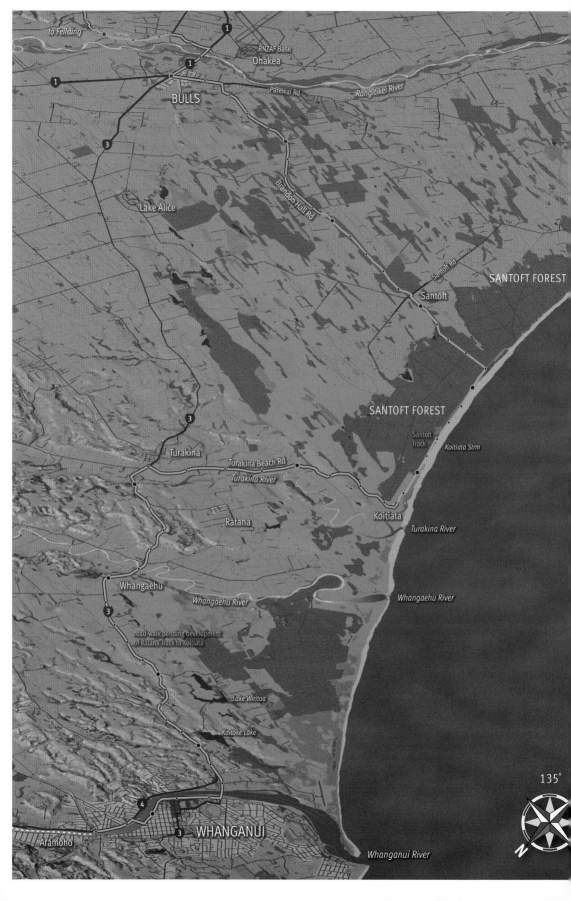

to Feilding

1

RNZAF Base
Ohakea

Parewai Rd

Rangitikei River

BULLS

1

1

3

Lake Alice

Brandon Hall Rd

SANTOFT FOREST

Santoft Rd

Santoft

3

SANTOFT FOREST

Santoft
Track

Koitiata Strm

Turakina

Turakina Beach Rd

Turakina River

Koitiata

Ratana

Turakina River

Whangaehu

Whangaehu River

Whangaehu River

3

road walk pending development
of Ratana Track to Koitiata

Lake Wiritoa

Kaitoke Lake

4

Aramoho

3

WHANGANUI

Whanganui River

135°

N

THE MAP SHOWS the trail from Whanganui to Koitiata as a road-walk, and so it is, but Te Araroa Trust and Te Araroa Whanganui Trust are working on finalising access and plans for the trail to come down the coastline from Whanganui, bridge the Whangaehu River and then go either via Ratana Pa or along the coastline through to Koitiata. The track can't yet be mapped, but it's already named itself for the enormously influential events which have occurred along this route.

In March 1918 a local farmer, Tahupotiki Wiremu Ratana, then aged 45 — an ordinary man, a smoker, a drinker — was camped on the coastline between the Whangaehu and Turakina rivers when the rolling waves suddenly disgorged two whales onto the beach. One died quickly, still clean and sleek. The other lived on, thrashing its distress in the black sands for hours until it too died.

Ratana embedded a vertebra from each of the whales on his farmhouse gateposts. He rendered down the whales' oil, and it would later be burned at ceremonies that heralded the most powerful Maori religious and political movement New Zealand had yet seen.

In 1918 the world was apocalyptic. The enormous blood sacrifice of World War I finished just as Spanish flu swept in, picking away at Maori. A cloud came in from the west, speaking to Ratana of leadership for Maori and renewal. *Destroy the Tohunga. Cleanse yourself.* Ratana seemed invested with the power to heal, at first within his family circle, then outside it. His reputation grew, too. He turned his farmland into a community for morehu — the tribal fragments — and the village of Ratana Pa grew. His followers pressed for a formal church and Ratana reflected on the two whales.

The one which had presented cleanly symbolised his spiritual mission, which would be biblically based, and safeguard souls. He designed a Ratana church with two square towers and on the towers, taken from the Book of Revelation, was a description of the Son of God: Arepa the first and Omeka the Last.

The second whale had thrashed in pain. At what was now the headquarters of Ratana, the prophet built a meeting house, Te Manuao — the Man of War. The twin towers were set low and wide here, with a veranda stretching some 40 m between. This was the movement's political side, where the korero and the hui would take place, planning for a pan-tribal Maori renaissance, and the protection of Maori land.

RATANA TRACK	
NORTHERN START	Whanganui
SOUTHERN END	Koitiata
DISTANCE	Approximately 28 km
MAPS	60, 61, 62
TRACK STANDARD	Tramping

SANTOFT TRACK

NORTHERN START	Koitiata
SOUTHERN END	Bulls
DISTANCE	27 km
MAPS	62, 63, 64
TRACK STANDARD	Easy tramping

FOLLOW THE TRACK out to the beach and head south. Seven kilometres on, a Te Araroa bollard turns you inland to the small settlement of Santoft. LINZ topo maps continue to mark the 1884 wreck of the *Fusilier* just beyond this beach turnoff point, but don't rely on it as a landmark. The local wisdom is that the wreck was used for shelling practice during World War II, and whatever is left got covered over by sand.

The coast here is notoriously windblown, and you're heading inland across some of New Zealand's most extensive sand lands and sand forests. The pines that begin here and stretch for 60 km south were originally planted during Depression days to safeguard farmland and roads from the encroaching dunes. Then, in the 1950s, the Forest Service extended such shelter-belt planting to full-scale production forestry. The Santoft Forest you'll walk through was the first of the big new plantations — radiata pine, planted for its rapid growth, its tolerance of salt and wind and its ability to thrive on sandy soils. The forest is run by Ernslaw One, a Malaysian-owned company, which has permitted access through.

Continue along the forest road for 5 km, turn right at Santoft Rd and 60 m on there's an entrance left onto another forest track that leads away 5.5 km to link with Brandon Hall Rd. Follow the road for 8 km until it turns into Parewai Rd through to Bulls, a State Highway 1 town with a penchant for puns. The church with the motto Forgive-a-bull, the doctor's rooms Treat-a-bull, the antique store Collect-a-bull . . . so it goes.

Walk down State Highway 1 and cross the bridge over the Rangitikei River.

ough-tramper Nicky Gibson on Santoft Track.

ch turnoff to Santoft.

AT THE FIRST JUNCTION past Bulls Bridge, turn left down Wightman Rd and continue along 30 m past the Hurst Rd intersection to a stile alongside a double gate. From here, the route crosses private farmland for over 2 km, parallel to the river, before ascending the river terrace again, following a fence line with excellent views of the Rangitikei River and along the edge of a pine plantation to a short farm lane leading onto Ngaio Rd extension. Follow straight along, past crossroads where the Ohakea Radar Station is a prominent marker, to Mt Lees Scenic Reserve. The garden here is open to the public and was gifted to the people of New Zealand by Ormond Wilson, scholar and social activist.

Wilson was born in Bulls, but his academic abilities were recognised early and he was sent south as a boarder to Christ's College in Christchurch then on to Oxford University, where he graduated in 1930. That same year he inherited the 405 hectare Mt Lees Station from his grandfather. He stood as the Labour Party candidate for Rangitikei in 1935 and became the youngest MP in the first Labour government 1935–38. He failed to retain the seat at the next election and left New Zealand, becoming a BBC journalist, but returned to work at Mt Lees in the mid-1940s, and to stand successfully as Labour MP for Palmerston North 1946–49. He then left parliamentary politics to work with his wife Rosamund back at Mt Lees.

He became chairman of the Historic Places Trust from 1958, developing a deep interest in Maori history, and walkers who've come through the Te Porere redoubts will recognise some of his work. Wilson took the lead and personally worked on clearing and restoring the redoubts. In 1972 the Wilsons gave their Mt Lees homestead and the 12 hectares of bush garden they'd established there to the Crown. They moved to Wellington where both continued in active civic roles.

The Mt Lees homestead does morning and afternoon teas, and has rooms available. The route beyond stays on Ngaio Rd to turn briefly right into Mt Stewart–Halcombe Rd, left into Lees, through to Sandon Rd, and just before town, right into Ranfurly Rd, which leads through to the suburbs of Feilding. Turn right at West St, left into South St and go through to Kowhai Park, where you'll see the prominent clock tower that guides you in to the town centre.

FEILDING ROUTE

NORTHERN START	Bulls Bridge
SOUTHERN END	Feilding
DISTANCE	19 km
MAPS	64, 65
TRACK STANDARD	Easy tramping
CLOSURES	The farm section of this route is closed June 1–October 30. Alternative access is then via Hurst and Wilson roads. No dogs, firearms or vehicles are permitted on the farm.

BUNNYTHORPE ROUTE

NORTHERN START	Feilding
SOUTHERN END	Palmerston North
DISTANCE	22 km
MAPS	65, 66
TRACK STANDARD	Easy tramping

EXIT FEILDING on the combined cycleway–walkway over the Oroua River, and turn left 300 m beyond the bridge. Cross the main trunk line, turn right onto Campbell Rd and follow along to Bunnythorpe.

The footpath through Bunnythorpe passes the old Glaxo factory. GlaxoSmithKline is presently the third largest pharmaceuticals company in the world, and lists the origins of the Glaxo part of its name to 'the colonial New Zealand of 1873. Local entrepreneur Joseph Nathan established a trading company in Wellington that was a forerunner to the milk powder operation at Bunnythorpe, Manawatu.' In 1904 Nathan built the Glaxo factory here which pioneered powdered milk and baby food production in New Zealand. The company expanded successfully later into vitamins made from fish oil and other pharmaceuticals, but this factory is remembered mainly for its invention and production of Farex, the baby food that gave many New Zealanders a solid start.

Turn onto Stony Creek Rd before turning right at Clevelly Line back towards the railway line, following along Sangsters Rd parallel to the railway as it tails out onto farmland and a succession of stiles. The track now leaves the railway line to cut directly south on Roberts Line for 4 km to cross Kelvin Grove Rd into Lydia Place, a cul-de-sac, to pick up Roberts Line again, cross another railway line and end at State Highway 3. Directly across State Highway 3, Te Matai Rd, and then Riverside Drive, lead down to a fenced right-of-way to the Riverside Walkway. The 6 km stroll beside the Manawatu River leads through to the Fitzherbert Bridge, and from there it's a 2 km walk into the city's main square.

Volunteer Malcolm Prince installs a stile on the Bunnythorpe Route.

The Square, Palmerston North.

to Otaki Forks

TARARUA RANGE

Ohau River

Gladstone Rd

Gladstone

LEV

Poads Rd

Makahika Outdoor
Pursuits Centre

Poulton Rd

Arapaepae Lookout Track
to Levin

Makahika Ridge

Mangahao–Makahika
Track

Pt 657

Mangahao Upper
No 1 Reservoir

Blackwood Strm

Mangahao Lower
No 2 Reservoir

Tokomaru
No 3 Reservoir

Mangahao Rd

Mangahao
Power Stn

Shannon

Mangahao Rd

Manawatu River

Tokomaru Valley road-end

Tokomaru River

Makerua

Burtton's
old whare

Burttons Track

Tokomaru River

Tokomaru

Gordon
Kear
Forest

Back Track

Scotts Rd

Black Bridge

Turitea
Route

Linton

Manawatu River

Kahuterawa Rd

Greens Rd

Kahuterawa Rd

Linton Military
Training Camp

Longburn

Ngahere Rd

Old West Rd

218°

Turitea Walkway

Massey
University

Bledisloe Park

Turitea

Tennent Dr
Fitzherbert Bridge

Riverside
Walkway

PALMERSTON NORTH

FOLLOW TENNENT DRIVE around to Bledisloe Park and pick up the Turitea Walkway with its fine views over the Massey University campus, through to Old West Rd. The Upper Turitea Walkway leads into Ngahere Park Rd and from there enters the Turitea green corridor for 3 km before it changes to Greens Rd and descends through open farmland to Kahuterawa Rd. Follow along for 5 km to the Kahuterawa Recreation Hub. Walk up to Black Bridge and the start of the Back Track, a former road, closed in the 1960s, climbing steeply 200 m in just over 2 km, to reach the Scotts Rd road-end. The final 2 km along Scotts Rd leads to the Burttons Track entry at Gordon Kear Forest.

TURITEA ROUTE

NORTHERN START	Fitzherbert Bridge
SOUTHERN END	Burttons Track
DISTANCE	26 km
MAPS	66, 67
TRACK STANDARD	Easy tramping

THE TRACK IS NAMED for James Burtton, a farmer who in 1908 bought a cheap backblocks farm in the Tokomaru Valley. The farm lacked access but road reserve was already pegged out along the Tokomaru River, and Burtton hoped the local council would do the job. The council would not, so along with the struggle to stay provisioned, the bush clearances on his farm, the fencing, the sheep shearing and dipping, Jim Burtton also began work to secure his access along the rugged river valley. Using gelignite and a cold chisel to tap holes for the explosives, he blasted around the bluffs, then moved forward with pick and shovel. In the years through to 1915 he completed a dray track, 1.8 m wide and 4.8 km long, joining with Tokomaru Valley Rd and connecting to Shannon.

BURTTONS TRACK

NORTHERN START	Gordon Kear Forest
SOUTHERN END	Mangahao Rd
DISTANCE	17 km
MAPS	67, 68
TRACK STANDARD	Tramping

The track starts on forest road for the first 6 km before dropping steeply to a first stream crossing above the Tokomaru River. If this stream is running high, the Tokomaru River a little further on will be uncrossable.

The track crosses a second side stream, then the Tokomaru River, normally a knee-deep wade, but dangerous after heavy rain. It continues on private land along the Tokomaru's true left bank — the owners have specified no firearms, and leashed dogs only — then re-crosses the river to Burtton's old whare site. From here you're walking on the original Burttons Track out to Tokomaru Valley Rd.

The lonely tale of the backblocks farmer ends sadly. The swing bridge he'd put in across the river near the whare was in use for over 10 years, but became increasingly rickety. On March 15 1941, the wire rope holding one side of the bridge broke and tipped Jim Burtton 8 m onto the rocks below. With a badly broken leg, broken ribs and internal injuries, the farmer hauled himself out along his track to a neighbour 6.5 km distant. He died in Palmerston North Hospital that same night, aged 60.

Walk up Tokomaru Valley Rd to Mangahao Rd, turning right for access out to Shannon, or left for 2 km, past the Tokomaru No. 3 Reservoir. The Makahika Track entrance is 800 m past the reservoir, on the right.

MANGAHAO– MAKAHIKA TRACK

NORTHERN START	Mangahao Rd
SOUTHERN END	Poulton Rd
DISTANCE	15 km
MAPS	68, 69
TRACK STANDARD	Tramping

THE TRACK CLIMBS to a low spur, where you'll see a destination board with maps and estimated times. It stays high, then descends to cross three tributaries of the Blackwood Stream, before climbing to the highest point on the trail, 5 km in, Pt 657, with sweeping views over the Horowhenua out to Kapiti Island.

The track follows the Makahika Ridge then descends past Archey's Lookout, dropping quickly down to the old tram terminus of the Bartholomew Timber Company. The company once logged native timber on these hills and the track uses the old benched route through bush, crossing the Makahika Stream, then follows a poled route across private farmland to the stile at Poulton Rd.

The Makahika Outdoor Pursuits Centre 2 km down Poulton and Gladstone roads is a possible stopover, but you'll need to book before leaving Palmerston North — it's often full. If you need to go straight to Levin for resupply, the entrance to the 7.5 km Arapaepae Lookout Track into Levin heads off right 300 m before the Makahika Centre. To reach the next Te Araroa track start, go 3.5 km down Gladstone Rd and turn right into Poads Rd.

Burtton (standing fourth from left) and members of the Manawatu Tramping Club.

ff Chapple with the track's new DOC sign.

wellington

Wellington from Mt Kaukau.

THE LAND

The Wellington landscape is youthful, rugged, and riven with fault lines. East to west the land is slowly compressing — the rub of the subducting Pacific Plate pushing everything up, tilting it west and stretching it south, jolt by jolt. Some time or another, this part of the country has it in for us.

Te Araroa meantime takes happy advantage of the terrain. The trail tramps across the austere Tararua ridges, through tussock, leatherwood, and soft cloud forest, stays high and generally ignores the fault lines until it comes down across the green flank of Tinakori Hill into Wellington itself. Then there's the one you can't ignore. Tinakori Hill is one eroded side of the famous Wellington Fault that runs straight through the city, and as you step off the hill onto St Mary St and cross Glenmore St headed for the Wellington Botanic Garden, you're stepping onto a crack that can, in a single moment, suddenly drop you 2 m and move you 3 m south. Those were the vertical and lateral movements the last time the Wellington fault moved, around 500 years ago, and when it fractures again some time over the next few hundred years, Wellington has its fingers crossed that the movement is no greater than that. In 1855, the Wairarapa Fault just 30 km east of the city fractured laterally 17 m in some places, and 6.5 m vertically in a magnitude 8.2 earthquake.

THE PEOPLE

Ninety-six days out from Plymouth, on August 16 1839, William Wakefield sighted New Zealand from the three-masted barque *Tory* and noted Mt Ruapehu erupting in the north. The *Tory* headed for Cook Strait.

Wakefield had come to buy land for the first 900 immigrants organised by the New Zealand Company, and he wanted it quickly, before the British government established sovereignty over New Zealand and brought Maori land sales under Crown control. In September 1839, Te Ati Awa chiefs duly signed Wakefield's Deed of Settlement for Wellington and the *Tory* fired a triumphant 21-gun salute.

Hardly had the echoes rolled back from the hills than Wakefield began to suspect it might not be so easy. Three weeks later, the *Tory* sailed up to Kapiti Island. Wakefield's meeting with Ngati Toa chief Te Rauparaha was given dread dimension by a Ngati Raukawa raid that had just left Te Ati Awa mourning 16 dead. The Ngati Toa chief was not happy with the unauthorised settlement at the bottom end of his domain. His followers grimaced at the Englishman, and threatened to descend on Wellington.

Thus Wellington, then and now: always conscious of the barbarians beyond its gates but an entirely self-assured city; cupped by its hills, prepared for the big shake with its New Zealand-invented base isolators under the big buildings; an intelligent city, but romantic also with its crooked pathways, its town belt, its Aeolian sculptures, its live theatre, and, in Miramar, its fantastic computer-generated images.

It helms the nation from the Beehive. One in eight of its workers is a public servant turning political will into carefully controlled national policy. Maybe that's why Wellingtonians were the very first New Zealanders to organise and tramp their considerable backyard. They did it in the 1920s and they do it still, senior civil servants amongst them, perhaps needing the Tararuas as a wilderness sufficient to mock the very idea of control.

THE TARARUA RANGE is the North Island's oldest and many would say its ultimate tramping ground. From the Tararua tops, khaki ridges tunnel away south towards Wellington, and distant South Island summits chisel the sky.

The Tararua ridges are exhilarating, but they can also be dangerous, with sudden weather changes, snow in any season, high winds, and clouds that can occlude the poled track and signage. Trampers should take maps and be able to read them. They should get a three- or four-day weather report before starting, take enough food to wait out bad weather in the huts, and be prepared to return to the huts if strong winds and weather close in when starting a new section.

This summary divides the tramp into three one-day stages. Each stage has a hut roughly mid-way, allowing stopovers that can turn any one-day tramp into an easier two-day section, but at the risk of a longer tramp being more subject to weather change. Hut and summit heights are noted, also distances, and timings that indicate where steep terrain slows tramping times. Timings are approximate only.

1) Poads Road to Te Matawai Hut. The tramp up the ridge track to the 18-bunk Waiopehu Hut (960 m) is in bush cover throughout. (Distance 10 km, time 4 hours.) The track onward climbs Waiopehu (1094 m) and Twin Peak (1097 m), where there's a memorial for a tramper killed in a 1936 storm, to Richards Knob (985 m), then descends, bearing right at the first track intersection, to Butcher Saddle (690 m). It bears right again at the next track intersection, climbing to Te Matawai Hut (900 m), which has a helipad. (Distance 6 km, time 4 hours.)

2) Te Matawai Hut to Nichols Hut. The track climbs steeply from Te Matawai to break out of the bushline and ascend Pukematawai (1432 m), then descends to the two-bunk Dracophyllum Hut (1100 m). (Distance 8 km, time 4–5 hours.) It climbs again to Puketoro (1152 m), then at the next high point, Kelleher (1182 m), watch for a cairn that marks where the track zigzags down a steep ridge, back to the bushline. Follow along an undulating ridge that rises to Nichols (1242 m). Within 200 m of the descent from the summit, Nichols Hut is to the east (left) below the track line. You could miss it in poor weather. (Distance 5 km, time 4 hours.)

TARARUAS TRACK

NORTHERN START	Poads Rd
SOUTHERN END	Otaki Forks
DISTANCE	47 km
MAPS	69, 70, 71
TRACK STANDARD	Hard tramping

3) Nichols Hut to Otaki Forks. Follow the ridge up the summit of Mt Crawford (1462 m) for great views of the Tararua Range stretching ahead, the South Island, Kapiti Island, and possibly Mt Taranaki. Descend to Junction Knob (1375 m), turn right at the junction to Shoulder Knob (1310 m) where the track re-enters the bush, and descend steeply to cross the Otaki River on a swing bridge through to Waitewaewae Hut. (Distance 8 km, time 4 hours.) From Waitewaewae Hut (100 m) ascend to the Plateau (530 m), then descend to Saddle Creek (200 m), and cross the Otaki Forks swing bridge to the car park. (Distance 10 km, time 4 hours.) Parawai Lodge (12 bunks) is sited before this bridge, and there's a DOC warden located near the overnight car park with a phone to offer assistance if needed.

Walk 2 km up to Schoolhouse Flat where there's a standard camping ground.

PUKEATUA TRACK

NORTHERN START	Fenceline car park
SOUTHERN END	Mangaone South Rd road-end
DISTANCE	14 km
MAPS	71, 72
TRACK STANDARD	Tramping

THE FENCELINE CAR PARK is 200 m north of the Schoolhouse Flat camp. Follow the Fenceline Loop Track for 700 m before a sharp turn uphill onto a southwest ridge. The track then ascends through mixed forest with grassy clearings en route that give wide views of Otaki Forks and the Tararua Range.

The track breaks out of the bushline to skirt low scrub towards the Pukeatua summit, offering wide views out over the Kapiti Coast, Kapiti Island and the top of the South Island. It follows a broad ridge west off the summit, then quickly sheds 300 m of altitude within 2 km. You then cross over into covenanted land whose owners, the Carters, have generously allowed access. Beyond, you enter onto avenues of old pine, before dropping to a stream and an old four-wheel-drive track out, across a swing bridge to Mangaone South Rd road-end.

Follow the quiet Mangaone South Rd into Ngatiawa Rd, into Reikorangi Rd and into Waikanae.

Tararuas and Pukeatua Tracks

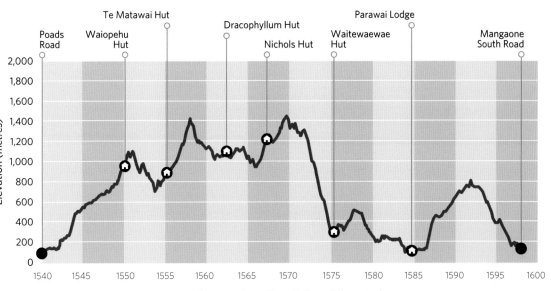

Elevation profile showing distance from Cape Reinga (kilometres) from 1540 to 1600, with the following labelled points: Poads Road, Waiopehu Hut, Te Matawai Hut, Dracophyllum Hut, Nichols Hut, Waitewaewae Hut, Parawai Lodge, Mangaone South Road.

Distance from Cape Reinga *(kilometres)*

Trampers ascending Mt Crawford, Tararuas Track.

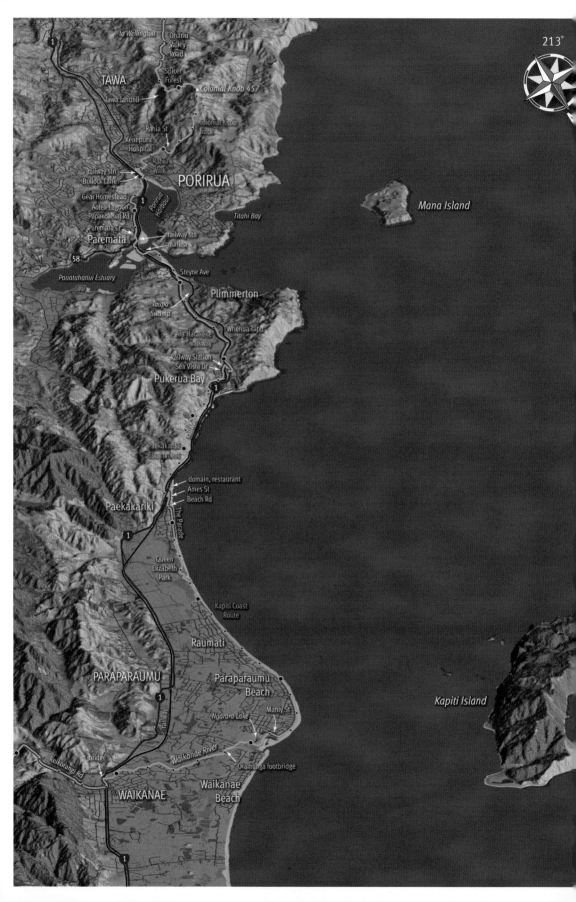

AT THE WAIKANAE RIVER BRIDGE on State Highway 1, take the track down the river's true right bank, then cross south on the Otaihanga footbridge. Follow the riverbank west towards the coast and join the track and boardwalk through the Waikanae Estuary Scientific Reserve, exiting onto Manly St. From Manly St, follow the grass verge down until the boardwalk takes you to the beach.

Head along the beach to Paekakariki. You'll find beachfront cafés en route and the first full view of Kapiti Island. This steep island has influenced the whole western coast. Its currents have pulled out the sandy promontory you're now walking, and it's also been a natural fortress for Maori, attacked and won by Ngati Toa in the early 1820s and a base for Te Rauparaha's control of the western coast. His bones are there, and now the island is a nature reserve.

Turn onto Queen Elizabeth Park's undulating coastal track then, about 1.5 km along, take a sealed Whareroa Rd 100 m inland. Turn right at the next intersection and follow along another 100 m before rejoining the unsealed coastal track to the end of the park. Continue along The Parade for 2 km then turn left into Beach Rd, Paekakariki's main street.

KAPITI COAST TRACK

NORTHERN START	Waikanae River Bridge
SOUTHERN END	Paekakariki
DISTANCE	22 km
MAPS	72, 73
TRACK STANDARD	Easy tramping

From Beach Rd, where a bar, cafés and store cater to all needs, head south down Ames St to State Highway 1. There, turn north across the railway overbridge and descend the stairs on the north side of the bridge, where the concrete path takes you safely onto the start of the escarpment.

The first part of the track meanders alongside the railway and highway, through small patches of trees, where already the birdlife is noticeable. An old quarry offers a glimpse at the history of the area and the signage along the route is informative and interesting.

Having dropped back alongside the railway to edge around a bluff, walkers then reach the 'moment of truth' — a series of staircases signalling the start of a long and steady climb to the highest point of the track.

The rewards are immense at the top — extensive views over the Kapiti Coast, to the South Island and, on a very clear day, to Taranaki and Ruapehu. From this high point a steep set of steps descends and the track weaves around the side of the escarpment, taking walkers through kohekohe forest and the extensive birdlife that call it home.

PAEKAKARIKI ESCARPMENT TRACK

NORTHERN START	Paekakariki
SOUTHERN END	Pukerua Bay
DISTANCE	10 km
MAPS	73, 74
TRACK STANDARD	Tramping

Another breathtaking set of steps delivers walkers to the first of two majestic swing bridges that have made this track enormously popular and well-known in the region — putting the exclamation mark on Te Araroa's most expensive and ambitious project to date.

The track rejoins the railway for the final stretch around into Pukerua Bay, ending at the Pukerua Bay railway station for a convenient trip home. Through-walkers can cross the State Highway 1 pedestrian bridge to continue south.

ARA HARAKEKE WALKWAY

NORTHERN START	Pukerua Bay
SOUTHERN END	Paremata Railway Station
DISTANCE	9 km
MAPS	74
TRACK STANDARD	Easy tramping

THIS VERY PLEASANT paved walkway is marked through with red and white posts. It starts from the Pukerua Bay shops on State Highway 1, and leads away downhill past the Whenua Tapu cemetery. It flattens out past the large Taupo Swamp, where you may see, unsurprisingly, the New Zealand swamp hen or pukeko, ducks, and maybe a heron.

Follow along to the railway underpass onto Steyne Ave. Just before the road crosses the Main Trunk Line, the walkway turns right to follow the coast to the marina. It ducks under the railway at the south end of the marina complex, and crosses the Pauatahanui Estuary mouth on the Paremata Bridge. The track then leads away into the Paremata Railway Station car park.

A pedestrian overbridge crosses State Highway 1 from the station car park onto Paremata Cres, which changes into Papakowhai Rd as you head south. Follow along to Aotea Lagoon. Exit this waterside reserve to the south, cross Whitford Brown Ave and turn briefly right into Okowai Rd. Go through the historic Gear Homestead grounds and onto a track leading onto the State Highway 1 corridor. A path leads off from there to the motorway offramp into Porirua. Turn left into Bullock Lane to the railway station. Porirua — previously a village on an estuary — was built to a plan in the 1960s, and the ease of entry into the city reflects the 1960s concern that people should move freely around the city. As you pass through you'll see a city spaciously designed for easy pedestrian movement.

iti Island from Queen Elizabeth Park's coastal dunes, Kapiti Coast Track.

kakariki Escarpment Track.

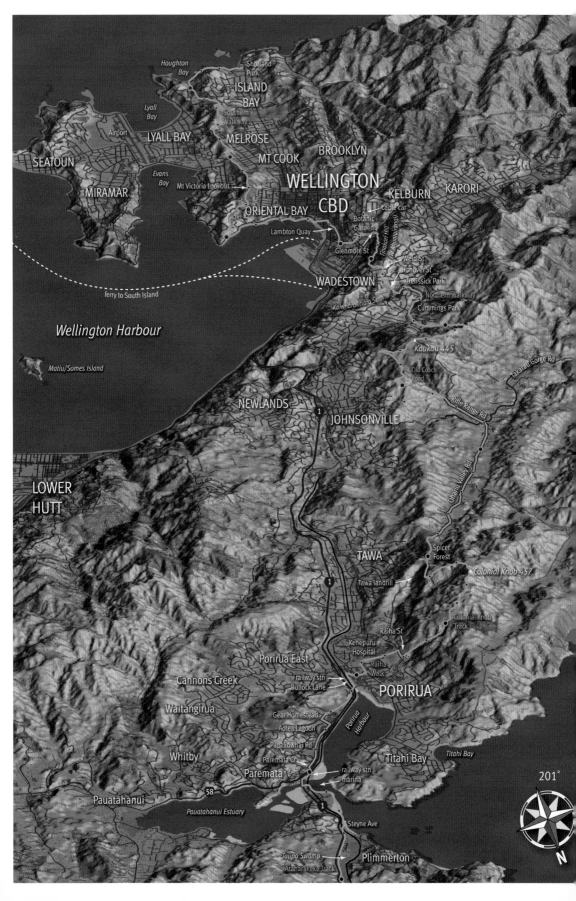

IN 2000 Porirua City's Raiha Walk became the first Te Araroa walk to be constructed through a city precinct — it's special. You'll see embedded in its bollards the first Te Araroa symbols ever struck.

The track is short, but you'll walk a dappled path under trees, cross an elegant footbridge and go past the sweeping stone steps of the former Porirua Lunatic Asylum — damaged in the Wairarapa earthquakes of 1942, demolished and replaced by the Kenepuru General Hospital. The track leads out onto Raiha St. Turn right and 200 m down the road the Colonial Knob Track begins.

RAIHA WALK

NORTHERN START	Hagley St
SOUTHERN END	Raiha St
DISTANCE	1.5 km
MAPS	74
TRACK STANDARD	Easy tramping

COLONIAL KNOB is the highest hill around Porirua, and the well-benched track climbs a crooked 4.5 km to the summit (459 m). You can look straight across at the South Island, here confirming its considerable over-ride onto North Island latitudes. Closer in is the last bit of rugged North Island west coast, through to Makara's beach settlement, and the windfarm beyond.

Leaving the summit, watch for the white poles with yellow circles that lead you south over farmland and across a stile into Spicer Forest. Methane from the Tawa landfill far below sometimes drifts uphill here, and black-backed gulls glide above, but the track through Spicer is a pleasant, grassed, wide ridge through forest. Wellington city plans an outer green belt that will extend in this part of the world from Mt Kaukau 7 km through to Colonial Knob, now behind you, along the farmed ridge just ahead. Agreement is not yet secured, however, so Te Araroa now turns steeply downhill through pines to exit onto the Ohariu Valley Rd road-end.

Ohariu Valley Rd does not have a wide shoulder, so be watchful for infrequent cars. Walk through to the intersection where Ohariu Valley Rd turns sharp left, and go straight ahead up Rifle Range Rd. At the road-end, signage takes you onto the old coach road across the southern flank of Mt Kaukau. Near the Mt Kaukau summit, Te Araroa diverts off this old route, onto Wellington city's Northern Walkway.

COLONIAL KNOB TRACK

NORTHERN START	Raiha St
SOUTHERN END	Ohariu Valley Rd
DISTANCE	7 km
MAPS	74, 75
TRACK STANDARD	Tramping

NORTHERN WALKWAY

NORTHERN START	Mt Kaukau
SOUTHERN END	Botanic Garden
DISTANCE	7 km
MAPS	75
TRACK STANDARD	Tramping

MT KAUKAU'S 445 m summit is Wellington's natural watchtower and keep. From up here you can spot the interisland ferries that ply the circular harbour below, and the jets that slant up from the airport. From here it's easy to see the town belt — Wellington's green corridor that frames the city — standing above the city's original inner suburbs and its CBD.

The track descends Kaukau to the south, and exits through Cummings Park. It follows streets through to Trelissick Park, descending sharply to pick up the Kaiwharawhara Stream and follow it through to an exit at Hanover St. Wadestown suburb then hosts the walkway through to an entry off Weld St into Wellington's town belt, then the track descends the side of Tinakori Hill with wide views across the city. It exits at St Mary St, and heads up Glenmore St to the red-brick Founders Gates into the Botanic Garden. Follow the signage up the hill and through Wellington's most beautiful park to the cable-car terminus.

WELLINGTON

NORTHERN START	Cable-car terminus
SOUTHERN END	Island Bay
DISTANCE	14 km
MAPS	75
TRACK STANDARD	Easy tramping

FROM THE CABLE CAR, the route descends through the Wellington Botanic Garden and historic Mount Street Cemetery to New Zealand's parliament — known locally as 'the Beehive'.

Then it's along Wellington's 'Golden Mile' shopping strip and through Civic Square to the stunning waterfront, past Te Papa (New Zealand's national museum) and around Oriental Bay.

The route then climbs Mt Victoria, enjoying views across Wellington city, and follows the Southern Walkway.

Descending into Houghton Bay, the final walk along Wellington's south coast gives a peaceful opportunity to reflect on the journey to date, before crossing Shorland Park to Te Araroa's North Island foundation stone, unveiled by Sir Jerry Mateparae, Governor-General of New Zealand, at the trail opening on 3 December 2011. The stone bears a Maori blessing.

Kia tupato kia pai to hikoi
Me te titiro whanui, kia koa
Ki nga taonga kei mua i a koe

Walk the path in safety
Look deeply and learn
From your surroundings

iti Island from Colonial Knob, Colonial Knob Track.

nelson–marlborough

THE LAND

The Marlborough Sounds area at the top of the South Island was once rumpled hill and valley territory with rivers discharging south, but nothing stays the same. As Te Araroa goes down one of its arms, exploring the coves and intimate waterways, it treads a land that's sunk towards the northeast over millions of years and been inundated by the sea.

The trail crosses alluvial fans through Linkwater, and flat land on the approach to Havelock. That flat land is the beginning of the Kaituna Valley, a former riverbed where the southbound rivers of the rumpled top territory once met with the Pelorus, and turned south to join the Wairau River.

The trail follows the deep pools of the Pelorus River into the hills, then leaves it for the rigours of the Richmond Range. The Alpine Fault has wrenched the Richmond Range sideways and without a ridge system to follow, Te Araroa gains and loses height as it goes through it.

At the south end it follows around the ochre slug of the Red Hills. The Red Hills here are on the western side of the Alpine Fault; the Red Hills in Otago are on the eastern side. In the 1940s a maverick geologist, Harold Wellman, would snip geological maps along the Alpine Fault and slide one against the other to show the neat match. He'd draw his theory in beer suds to whatever audience would listen in West Coast bars. In 1949 he presented his evidence to a science congress in Christchurch to great interest and some incredulity — a slip-strike fault that could move mountain sections 460 km horizontally was not recognised anywhere else on earth. Tectonic-plate theory burst forth in the 1960s and gave Wellman a final vindication.

Beyond the Richmond Range lies the very beautiful tramping ground of the Nelson Lakes National Park.

Marlborough Sounds.

THE PEOPLE

Maori called these sounds Te Tau Ihu — evoking the carved prow of Maui's canoe within this filigreed coast. In December 1642 the two ships of Dutch explorer Abel Tasman encountered Maori canoes in Golden Bay, lost four sailors to a sudden attack, and sailed on. In January 1770 Captain James Cook sailed into the sounds with a Polynesian interpreter, and the interaction with Maori, aside from British alarm at cannibalism, was more respectful.

In August 1839 the New Zealand Company's ship *Tory* sailed in. William Wakefield cast an eye over land he found too steep, and sailed north to found Wellington. The company would revisit the top of the South Island, however, and in 1842 another brother, Captain Arthur Wakefield, was put in charge of the Nelson settlement.

George and Barbara Rutherford would arrive there in 1843. They began the Scottish line in New Zealand that gave the world Ernest, an amiable but precocious lad whose pen-nib is reputedly buried in the ceiling of the old Havelock schoolhouse, and who would go on, at the Cavendish Laboratory at Cambridge, to discover the atomic nucleus.

Nelson and Blenheim are the two main centres, each one vying year by year to be New Zealand's sunniest town. Nelson is renowned for its consistently powerful vernacular arts, and has its orchards. Blenheim has wide hectares of grapes and produces high-end wines from the stony Wairau Plains. Such industries, together with farming, and the entrepôt activities in Picton, are the mainstays of a prosperous region.

SOUTH-BOUND THROUGH-TRAMPERS will usually come across Cook Strait by interisland ferry, then travel up from Picton to Ship Cove by water taxi. It's a maritime break in the trail, but the North and South Islands overlap, and if the trail is gauged by continuous latitude, then there's no break. In fact, Wellington is at 41° 17' 20" and Ship Cove at 41° 05' 35" — a fifth of a degree north of the capital.

At Ship Cove, trampers begin one of New Zealand's longest, most popular and most serviced tracks. Campsites, lodges, and a hotel dot the route, and it has boats to transfer heavy packs from stop to stop. You can choose from many walking options, and there'll always be a handy campsite, or a side track to a lodge.

The trail begins at the Captain James Cook monument. Near the top of the monument, in brightly painted bas-relief, is a blue sailor's arm, truncated at the shoulder in the heraldic manner, brandishing the British flag. The banner beneath says 'Circa Orbem'. The British explorers were midway through a planned circumnavigation of the globe when they ghosted in to Ship Cove, but were also completing a six-month circumnavigation and mapping of New Zealand. Cook made a discovery here that thrilled him. Explorers like passages, straits, channels. They also pay attention to the clues explorers before them might have left in their logs.

One hundred and twenty-seven years before Cook's arrival, Abel Tasman had lost four men to a Maori attack in Golden Bay, and having up-anchored and sailed away north, his log noted a strong current pulling the *Heemskerk* towards what his log reported as a deep bay at 41° 51'. It was a note to intrigue any future mariner encountering an unmapped land. As Cook sailed the *Endeavour* deeper into the same bay, the strait still did not open before him, but Tasman's log, and instinct, had prepared him for something more. During their stay at Ship Cove, he and a small party took the pinnace and sailed across to Arapawa Island. Cook climbed Kaitepeha and would write in his journal 'I was abundantly recompenced for the trouble I had assending the hill for from it I saw what I took to be the Eastern Sea and a strait or passage from it into the Western Sea'. His name would be appended to this strait, and he would return to Ship Cove five times during his three Pacific voyages.

Joseph Banks, botanist aboard the *Endeavour*, called the birdsong here 'the most melodious wild music I have

QUEEN CHARLOTTE TRACK

NORTHERN START	Ship Cove
SOUTHERN END	Anakiwa
DISTANCE	71 km
MAPS	76, 77, 78
TRACK STANDARD	Tramping

ever heard', and as the track starts through beech forest you'll certainly hear the bellbirds, at their best when there are six or eight all talking at once. The track climbs almost immediately and from the first saddle the views stretch as far as Kapiti Island.

Twelve kilometres on from the start, after a second saddle and a descent onto the shoreline, you'll reach Furneaux Lodge, the most famous of the walk's stopovers, with backpacker as well as lodge accommodation. It's an old homestead of sufficient grace that it was once offered to the government as a prime-ministerial retreat.

The walk around to Camp Bay is mostly flat and coastal, with a definite temptation to stop in favour of the restaurant meals available at Punga Cove. The track then climbs to a central ridge and stays there for 22 km, high above the sounds, with water stops and shelters en

Through-tramper Nicky Gibson, Queen Charlotte Track, between Bay of Many Coves campsite and Black Rock campsite, looking west.

route, and side tracks down to waterfront lodges. At Torea Saddle, trampers usually take the 1 km side road to the Portage Resort Hotel, which has backpacker and more refined accommodation, a bar, a restaurant and café.

The track climbs steeply south of the saddle to pass the Queen Charlotte Track's highest point (407 m), descends sharply, then undulates away to end at Anakiwa, 20 km distant.

The track is wide and accommodates mountain bikes along its length for most of the year, but the bikes are off limits on the first 20 km section during high summer, December 1–February 28.

Note that private landowners en route have set up a $12 charge for access which can be paid at the Picton i-Site, on the water taxis that take you to Ship Cove, or at Furneaux Lodge.

LINK PATHWAY

STUDENTS FROM THE Anakiwa Outward Bound School helped build the Te Araroa extension from the south side of the settlement through to Queen Charlotte Drive.

The Link Pathway begins off Anakiwa Rd, just south of the settlement, and follows between the road and the shoreline to a junction with Queen Charlotte Drive. It then runs parallel to the drive towards the Mahakipawa Inlet, before a road-shoulder walk is needed until the path recommences near Belvue. Continue past Moenui and right around the peninsula on a restored bridleway and all the way into Havelock. The town is the centre of the green-lipped mussel industry, and the mussels are served here by people who do it well.

Walk just over 2 km from the edge of Havelock, where the main road meets the water, then take a right into Boultons Rd. Cross the river then take another right into Te Hoiere Rd across what is known locally as Twiddle's Island. Take a left at the T-junction into Kaiuma Bay Rd and follow that 10 km to Daltons Bridge, where Daltons Track commences and follows the true left of the river. Please DO NOT use the farm road as this is private farm property.

NORTHERN START	Anakiwa
SOUTHERN END	Havelock
DISTANCE	17 km
MAPS	78, 79
TRACK STANDARD	Tramping

DALTONS TRACK

THE TRACK STARTS at a stile to the left of Daltons Bridge. It follows the true left bank of the Pelorus River along a grazed pasture margin, through occasional barberry and other scrub. The track crosses two farms where access has been generously granted by the landowners, and walkers should stay on the track and respect the conditions of access on private land: no dogs, no guns, no camping and no entry after dark. It finally enters mixed podocarp and beech forest within the Pelorus Bridge Scenic Reserve and a serviced DOC campsite.

Walk up Maungatapu Rd to the start of the Pelorus River Track.

NORTHERN START	Daltons Bridge west end
SOUTHERN END	Pelorus Bridge
DISTANCE	7 km
MAPS	80
TRACK STANDARD	Tramping

225°

N

to Red Hills

take left fork

Tarn Hut

MT RICHMOND
FOREST PARK

Goulter River

Purple Top 1532

Mt Rintoul 1731

Little Rintoul 1643

Mt Rintoul Hut

R A N G E

Lee River

Old Man Hut

Old Man 1514

Slaty Peak 1344

Mt Starveall 1511

Ada Flat

Slaty Hut

Starveall Hut

Richmond Range
Alpine Track

Hacket Ck

R I C H M O N D

Mt Richmond 1756

Pelorus River

Hacket Junction

Hacket H

to Aniseed Valley

Browning Hut

Mt Fell 1599

Totara
Saddle

B R Y A N T

Roebuck Hut

Middy Creek Hut

R A N G E

Pelorus River
Track

Captain Creek Hut

MT RICHMOND
FOREST PARK

Maungatapu Rd
road-end

Rainy River

Pelorus River

Maungatapu Rd

FOR THROUGH-WALKERS, this track is the start of the long, 106 km tramp through the Richmond Range. It's also a stand-alone tramp, exiting from Hacket Junction to Aniseed Valley Rd above Nelson.

From the Maungatapu Rd road-end it's an easy 8 km tramp to Captain Creek Hut.

Five hundred metres beyond the hut the track crosses the unbridged Captain Creek. The creek has a big catchment, and can be dangerous after rain.

The track then crosses and re-crosses the Pelorus River on swing bridges over a river of pure greens and blues with trout in the pools, then heads for a high, dry ridge, and beyond it some root-ridden and rocky descents. There's three huts to choose from en route to Hacket Hut, so you can tramp at your own speed.

PELORUS RIVER TRACK

NORTHERN START	Maungatapu Rd road-end
SOUTHERN END	Hacket Junction or Hacket Hut
DISTANCE	31 km (Junction) or 32 km
MAPS	81, 82, 83
TRACK STANDARD	Tramping

THE RICHMOND RANGE is a long wilderness tramp offering the pleasures of height and solitude, and some attendant dangers. Most of it is a route. Once above the bushline it's generally marked only with poles or cairns. The track is often not defined, and is easy to lose in cloud. Routes are defined as 'suitable for fit, well-equipped people with a high degree of experience and with navigating and river-crossing experience'.

Typically the through-tramp will take five days, or if you've come in from the Maungatapu Rd road-end, eight days. Weather can change during that time, and you must be well prepared. The track goes over four high summits and sidles across the flanks of three other peaks — all above the bushline. Trampers should check the seven-day weather report, take enough food for extra days, and be prepared to wait out bad weather in the huts. It's preferable to tramp with a companion on this route and solo trampers must be sure of their skills.

Track summaries here divide the tramp into five one-day stages. Each stage has a hut roughly midway, allowing stopovers that can turn any one-day tramp into an easier two-day section, but as with the Tararuas, at the risk of the longer tramp being more subject to weather change. Hut and summit heights are noted, as are distances and timings to indicate where steep terrain slows tramping times.

RICHMOND RANGE ALPINE TRACK (STAGE 1)

NORTHERN START	Hacket Hut
SOUTHERN END	Rintoul Hut
DISTANCE	79 km total. This stage 24 km
MAPS	83
TRACK STANDARD	Tramping

1) Hacket Hut to Slaty Hut. The track is slippery along Hacket Creek with lots of crossings, then begins a 900 m climb through steadily dwarfing tree cover to Starveall Hut (1180 m) just above the bushline and with a natural garden of sub-alpine plants. (Distance 5.5 km, time 4 hours.) The route is then poled around the flanks of Mt Starveall before descending along a cut track through low beech to Slaty Hut (1400 m). (Distance 5.5 km, time 3 hours.)

2) Slaty Hut to Rintoul Hut. The tramping gets easier, with relatively gentle ascents and descents across tussock and scrub, views across a chasm to Mt Rintoul in the south, and a steep pull to the Old Man summit (1514 m). Just beyond the summit there's a water barrel. Two and a half kilometres beyond this summit there's a side track east, dropping steeply down to Old Man Hut (1100 m). (Distance 7.5 km [to the junction only, add a further 1 km for going to and from Old Man Hut], time 4 hours.)

The next leg is an encounter with deep scree. It's hard to maintain a good pace, and the poled route along a Little Rintoul ledge passes at one point a slight bulge in the rock wall above a drop-off. Beyond Little Rintoul (1643 m), the track drops nearly 200 m before climbing to the Mt Rintoul summit (1731 m), the track's highest point. The descent off Rintoul follows a gentle northwest ridge before heading steeply down to the bushline and Rintoul Hut. (Distance 5 km, time 6 hours.)

Pelorus River and Richmond Range Alpine Tracks

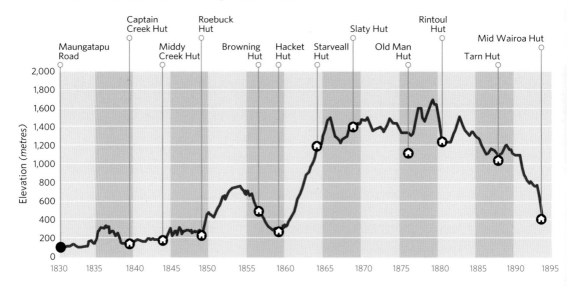

ough-trampers Nicky Gibson and Simon Cook, walking from Old Man summit towards Rintoul, Richmond Range Alpine Track.

ough-tramper Eyal Schwartz, Mt Rintoul summit, Richmond Range Alpine Track.

225°

N

to St Arnaud

63

Tophouse

Beebys Knob ▲

car park

Motupiko River

Kiki

Red Hills Hut 🏠

Maitland Ck

Beebys Ck

Richmond Range
Alpine Track

Motueka River (right)

Porters Creek Hut 🏠

Motueka River (right)

Motueka River (left)

R E D   H I L L S

Red Hill 1791

Hunters Hut 🏠

saddle

Mt Ellis 1615

Top Wairoa Hut 🏠

Wairoa River
(right)

MT RICHMOND
FOREST PARK

Richmond Range
Alpine Track

take right fork

Mid Wairoa Hut 🏠

Mt Patriarch 1656

Wairoa River (left)

Goulter River

Tarn Hut 🏠

take left fork

Purple Top 1532

MT RICHMOND
FOREST PARK

Mt Rintoul 1731

Little Rintoul 1643

Mt Rintoul Hut 🏠

Lee River

Old Man Hut 🏠

Wairau River

63

3) Rintoul Hut to Mid Wairoa Hut. The track leads off through beech forest on a wide ridge before climbing to Purple Top (1532 m). Two and a half kilometres on there's a track junction where you follow around left and head downhill another 3 km to Tarn Hut (1030 m), overlooking a near-circular tarn, and accessed off a short, steep side track. (Distance to the track junction 7.5 km, time 4 hours.) The track goes over a mild and forested summit, then takes the right fork at the next junction to begin an increasingly steep and rocky descent, with views through to the distant Red Hills, down to a swing-bridge crossing of the Wairoa River's east branch to Mid Wairoa Hut (370 m). (Distance 6 km, time 4 hours.)

If you need to bail from the Richmond Range at this point it's 10.5 km out to Wairoa Gorge Road, and a further 7.5 km before you'd find a house.

4) Mid Wairoa Hut to Hunters Hut. This is another rigorous section, following the Wairoa River's left branch to Top Wairoa Hut. If this small river is running high, the track is impassable, for there's a number of crossings, one at the head of a small waterfall. The track sometimes goes high above the watercourse, with a camber that may tilt you towards a drop-off, but nothing that sure feet can't handle. The last few kilometres of the walk are a shallow boulder-hop amongst rocks turned bright orange by crustose lichen and occasional green rock shards in the stream — serpentine. About now you will get your first close-up look at the Red Hills, and crest the riverbank to the Top Wairoa Hut (830 m). (Distance 7 km, time 5 hours.)

The Red Hills are highly unusual, a giant sliver of ophiolitic rock that mixes dark peridotites, serpentine, speckled gabbro, basalt, and abrasive crystals. It's full of minerals and ore, and it weathers to red. The hills are part of an ancient subducting plate that peeled away and lodged in the flank of Gondwana. Such remnants are rarely seen on land, and though this sliver runs practically the length of New Zealand, it's been unroofed in only a few places — jerked into the light here by the Alpine Fault. Plants can't cope with it: the beech forest stops at the foot of the hills, and plants that mat the lower flanks are often dwarfs.

The track climbs away from the hut across small seeps that are bitter to the taste. It climbs 2.5 km to a saddle then follows a steepening ridge of harsh, bare rock to pass just below the summit of Mt Ellis (1615 m) then descends through light forest cover to a crossing of the left branch of

RICHMOND RANGE ALPINE TRACK (STAGE 2)

NORTHERN START	Rintoul Hut
SOUTHERN END	State Highway 63
DISTANCE	79 km total. This stage 55 km.
MAPS	83, 84, 85, 86, 87
TRACK STANDARD	Hard tramping

the Motueka River. Remnants of the former Bush Edge Hut are visible here. DOC staffers Russell Griebel, Bob Waldie and Russell's dog Freckles died on duty when the hut was destroyed in 1995 by a flash flood. Hunters Hut (830 m) is at a safer 120 m above the river, and was built in 1997 as a memorial. (Distance 10.5 km, time 6 hours.)

5) Hunters Hut to Red Hills Hut. The scramble up and down loose rock as the track crosses side streams takes time, but it relents finally with a last gentle kilometre into the flatlands and swamp around Porters Creek Hut. (Distance 7 km, time 4 hours.) The ongoing track has similar harsh passages over rock and across streams 7 km through to a crossing of the right branch of the Motueka River, and follows along to where tussock begins to take hold, gentians bloom, and the weka may be out. Red Hills Hut (910 m) appears in the distance, and you've all but completed a substantial Richmond Range alpine crossing. (Distance 11 km, time 5 hours.)

From Red Hills Hut, a 5.5 km four-wheel-drive vehicle track zigzags steeply down to a derelict farmhouse on the flats, and an old cob cottage. A forest track takes you out a further 1 km to a car park and State Highway 63.

Turn right onto State Highway 63. The highway widens within a few kilometres to a good mown shoulder all the way to St Arnaud. The town is a busy centre to the tramping, camping, boating and baching community of the Nelson Lakes National Park, and resupply is easy here.

Richmond Range Alpine Track – continued

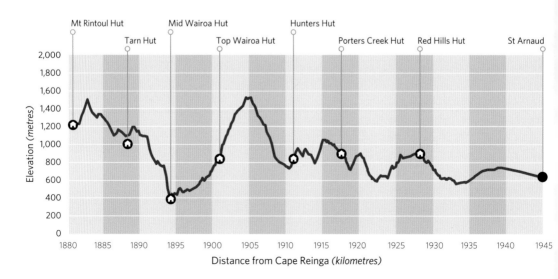

ough-tramper Nicky Gibson on the Red Hills, Richmond Range Alpine Track.

ough-tramper Simon Cook on the Richmond Range Alpine Track.

Belvedere Peak 2114

NELSON LAKES
NATIONAL PARK

Waiau
Pass

Lake Constance

Mt Franklin 2340

Waiau Pass
Track

Blue Lake

Blue Lake Hut

Kehu Peak 2220

Travers
Saddle

Mt Travers 2338

Sabine River (east)

Blue Lake
Track

MAHANGA RANGE

D'Urville River

Upper Travers Hut

Mt Cupola 2260

West Sabine Hut

Sabine River (west)

TRAVERS RANGE

Mt Hopeless 2278

Sabine River

ST ARNAUD RANGE

John Tait Hut

Travers/Sabine
Track

Lak
Rotoro

ROBERT RIDGE

NELSON LAKES
NATIONAL PARK

Travers River

Lakehead Hut

Lake Rotoiti

Kerr
Bay

63

St Arnaud
DOC Visitor Information Centre

Buller River

63

206°

N

ST ARNAUD IS THE GATEWAY to the Nelson Lakes National Park. The park has a network of spacious but popular huts, and the DOC area office here is very attuned to tramping needs. There's huge wall maps to study the way ahead, park maps for sale, and staff who know the routes and the incoming weather.

The Waiau Pass Route is a 113 km tramp that connects the Travers/Sabine Circuit and the Blue Lake Track north of Waiau Pass (1870 m) with the St James Walkway south of the pass. It's Te Araroa's second-highest saddle, and snowstorms can strike at any time. In spring and winter it's blocked by snow, and avalanche prone. On the good days of summer and early autumn it's the high point of an extraordinary tramp across the northern end of the Southern Alps.

This section gives only distances between huts, not formal timings, nor does it recommend distances for any tramping day. Te Araroa's route through the Nelson Lakes National Park and the St James Walkway is easier, prettier, and more social than its previous mountain sections, and tramping speeds are less critical. However, the track is long relative to the Tararuas route (61 km) and the Richmond Range route (77 km), and at Travers Saddle and Waiau Pass it turns from track to route standard — a poled route only, requiring good back-country skills, maps, and a high standard of gear.

1. St Arnaud to Lakehead Hut. From St Arnaud the track starts at the eastern end of Kerr Bay, Lake Rotoiti. It follows a shining lakefront through forest and resounding birdsong. Here DOC is ridding the forest of pests — you'll see often the wire mesh and wooden casings of a stoat trap with its enticing hen's egg. The bellbirds that chime here are a measure of DOC's success, but listen also for the harsh cry and musical whistles of the native parrot, kaka — nearly extinct in this forest but now returning. Lakehead Hut is about 15 minutes beyond the jetty at the top of the lake. (Distance 9 km.)

2. Lakehead Hut to John Tait Hut. The well-graded track continues up the river flats through open and forested sections to the hut named for John Tait, a former president of the Nelson Tramping Club who led the volunteer effort to fund and build a hut here in 1951. The original hut survived for 27 years

WAIAU PASS TRACK (STAGE 1)

NORTHERN START	St Arnaud
SOUTHERN END	Blue Lake Hut
DISTANCE	113 km total. This stage 42 km
MAPS	87, 88
TRACK STANDARD	Hard tramping

before replacement by this more substantial building with views out to Mt Travers and Mt Cupola. (Distance 12 km.)

3. John Tait Hut to Upper Travers Hut. The track continues more steeply now up the Travers Valley, crossing the Travers River on swing bridges and passing over winter avalanche paths. Upper Travers Hut is sited on a large flat at 1220 m, surrounded by a bewitching combination of beech, meadow, subalpine flowers and rocky knuckles protruding from low ground cover. (Distance 6 km.)

4. Upper Travers Hut to West Sabine Hut. The track continues as a well-defined ground trail marked with snow poles climbing 450 m to Travers Saddle (1787 m). Mt Travers summit (2338 m) stands off to the right, high enough to hold its summer snow patches. The saddle itself is an impressive crossing with tussock, alpine flowers, and cushion plants underfoot before the snow poles lead you onto a long skidding gravel face to the treeline. After crossing the east branch of the Sabine River in a chasm along the valley floor, the track climbs, sidles and then descends to the Sabine River's west branch and follows it up a short distance to West Sabine Hut. The whole traverse is apparently short, but can take six to eight hours, given the care needed to descend the gravel face. (Distance 8 km.)

5. West Sabine Hut to Blue Lake Hut. The track starts out through the dappled shade of beech, following a Sabine River that's sometimes wide and shallow and sometimes, as the track steepens, a tumbling cataract. It's bridged between reflective pools as it crosses a terrace near the top of the track, then begins a last steep pinch to Blue Lake Hut, to the source of the Sabine, and to Blue Lake itself, which is charming, very blue and very cold. (Distance 7 km.)

ravers from Travers Saddle, Waiau Pass Track.

Lake, Waiau Pass Track.

6. Blue Lake Hut to Upper Waiau Forks. This is the most demanding section of the Waiau Pass Route. It's a fair-weather route for experienced trampers or groups with experienced leaders. Trampers need to be fit, and reasonably agile.

The track leaves Blue Lake Hut through forest and climbs onto the moraine that dams Lake Constance. Snow poles mark a rough and rocky route parallel to the lake, then the track leads high along the bluffs on the western side, pushing through low grasses. A first encounter with the rigid, pointed leaves of wild Spaniard is possible here — it's the popular name for speargrass and it's one reason for wearing knee-high gaiters when tramping the South Island. The track scrambles downhill towards the lake head then continues across the valley floor for just over 500 m. You should then see a sign — Waiau Pass — pointing straight at the scree slope that rises steeply on your left.

Waratah markers lead away, and it's a direct climb straight up for the first kilometre, then a further 500 m sidle to the right. The pass overlooks the entire north of the South Island, and is a memorable lunch spot if the weather allows. Even in summer, you'll often find snow banks wedged amongst the rocks up here.

The route south of the pass leads on across rocky flats then begins a sharp descent, following waratah markers that seem wilted by heat but which are in fact twisted by the cold tonnages of winter avalanche. In places it's a hand-over-hand descent, but without exposure in the mountaineering sense of hanging out over a drop. The route reaches a sloping terrace then continues west before descending another bluff, to follow the west branch of the Waiau River down to its junction with the east branch. This is the Upper Waiau Forks, just under 3 km from the pass.

The tramp from Blue Lake Hut to Caroline Bivvy typically takes eight hours, and if you want to stop before that, look for the informal campsite at the Upper Waiau Forks. It's well sited, with water to hand, soft tent sites amidst beech forest, and the stone circles of many previous campfires. (Distance 8 km.)

7. Upper Waiau Forks to Caroline Bivvy. The track south from Upper Waiau Forks is now well marked through celery pine. It was put through in favour of Te Araroa two years ago, but the whole route through this valley is in fact an old greenstone trail used by southern Maori to

WAIAU PASS TRACK (STAGE 2)

NORTHERN START	Blue Lake Hut
SOUTHERN END	Anne River Hut
DISTANCE	113 km total. This stage 43 km.
MAPS	88, 89, 90
TRACK STANDARD	Hard tramping

bring West Coast jade through to an east-coast trade with the northern tribes. More recently the valley was part of St James Station's 78,000 hectare pastoral lease, but the Crown bought the lease in 2008, and two mountain ranges and the valleys between are now a conservation area that gives trampers unrestricted access and freedom to camp. The track leads through to Caroline Bivvy, a basic two-bunk shelter, and the last hut for a considerable distance. (Distance 5 km.)

8. Caroline Bivvy to Anne Hut. The tramp now gets fast and easy on the widening flats. Ghost forest stands either side of the valley — trees killed by the slow onset of coarse scree, and larger rockslides that occasionally spill out onto the grassland. The river braids, and you'll see matagouri shrubs, a spiny coloniser of dry places.

Nineteen kilometres on from the bivvy, the St James Station's Ada homestead sits on a raised terrace. It's privately owned, and trampers should give it a wide berth, and continue to the Ada River. In low to normal flows the river is a straightforward crossing. Te Araroa then links to the St James Walkway, a popular track where you'll meet other trampers.

The track crosses the Henry River by swing bridge but the first side-stream crossing beyond it can be dangerous in stormy weather, with a big catchment and a short, steep discharge into the river. The track continues on the true right of the Henry, then picks up a vehicle track through to a swing-bridge crossing of the Anne River. In July 2010 Anne River Hut was destroyed by fire. Its 20-bunk replacement is a serviced hut with heating and cooking facilities, making it a three-ticket or back-country Hut Pass stopover. (Distance 30 km.)

ough-tramper Alice Smith on Waiau Pass, Waiau Pass Track.

Hope Shelter

LAKE SUMNER
FOREST PARK

Hope River

to Windy
Point

to
Hanmer
Springs

Boyle River

7

Tui Track

Doubtful River

7

Boyle River

Mons Sex Millia 1835

POPLARS RANGE

Boyle
Village

Outdoor Education Centre

bridge

Faust 1710

7

Nina River

Boyle River

St James
Walkway

LIBRETTO RANGE

Lewis River

Magdalen Valley

bridge

Magdalen Hut

gorge

bridge

Boyle Flat Hut

Lewis
Pass

OPERA RANGE

Boyle River

Rokeby Hut

Anne
Saddle

Mt Jervois 1862

Anne River

bridge

Anne Hut

bridge

Waiau River

Henry River

Mt Federation 1612

St James
Walkway

214

Ada homestead

Ada River

Waiau River

N

9. Anne Hut to Boyle Flat Hut. As you strike out from Anne Hut, grazing cattle may watch you go, but they're sufficiently used to people that interest will be mild. Anne River begins to diminish, and the cattle flats finally give way to tussock, the river turns into a creek, and the track begins an easy climb through light beech forest to Anne Saddle. A steep descent takes you into the Boyle River Valley. Five and a half kilometres down the valley, Rokeby Hut provides a lunch spot on a terrace above the river, and cramped two-bunk overnight accommodation if you need it, and as a bivvy, it's free. The track continues downstream another 4 km to where a swing bridge across the river leads to the serviced Boyle Flat Hut — a three-ticket hut if you plan to overnight here. (Distance 15 km.)

10. Boyle Flat Hut to Boyle Village. Re-cross the swing bridge and the track south soon climbs the hillside to sidle high above a long gorge along forest paths made soft by leaf litter. It descends onto flats and reaches another swing bridge across the Boyle River. If you stay on the true left, there's a side trip here to Magdalen Hut just over 700 m distant — a very pleasant diversion if you're seeking a good lunch spot or stopover.

The main track crosses the swing bridge to gain the true right bank of the Boyle, and becomes a lengthy walk across grassy flats and through forest, with rock-hops across 11 side creeks that tumble off Faust Ridge, high above. The track crosses the Boyle again on a swing bridge and continues a further 2.5 km to the St James car park at Boyle Village adjacent to the Boyle River Outdoor Education Centre. (Distance 13 km.)

The Education Centre is run on behalf of schools in the Hurunui region. It's not always attended, and Boyle Village is only a collection of cribs, without shops. If through-trampers plan to use the centre as a food drop, or to take advantage of its backpacker accommodation on the way through, check before leaving St Arnaud that it's open on the date you plan to arrive. There's no cellphone coverage around Boyle Village. If you want to resupply, shuttle buses go through to Hanmer Springs, or you can hitchhike. The town is 57 km east, along State Highway 7 then turning left onto State Highway 7A, 48 km into the journey. Hanmer has everything necessary for resupply, including an outdoors shop, as well as cafés, restaurants, and hot pools.

WAIAU PASS TRACK (STAGE 3)

NORTHERN START	Anne Hut
SOUTHERN END	Boyle Village
DISTANCE	113 km total. This stage 28 km.
MAPS	90, 91, 92
TRACK STANDARD	Tramping

TUI TRACK

NORTHERN START	Boyle Village
SOUTHERN END	Harper Pass Track junction
DISTANCE	12 km
MAPS	92
TRACK STANDARD	Tramping

FROM THE ST JAMES CAR PARK at Boyle Village, the track follows markers to the highway and then continues on the landward side of the fence to a driveway leading to the old Boyle Base Hut. Cross State Highway 7 here, follow markers down to the Boyle River and ford it where indicated.

(Note: This river can be a problem after rain and if it can't be crossed safely at this point, back-track to State Highway 7, and continue south 10 km by road through to the car park at Windy Point. As you cross the stile here, you're entering the Lake Sumner Forest Park. This is the usual start point of the Harper Pass Track, and leads off to a swing bridge across the Boyle River.)

Assuming the Boyle River can be crossed safely, the Tui Track continues down the Boyle's true right bank on river flats to a confluence with Doubtful River. The Doubtful is also dangerous in high flows but can usually be crossed where marked a short distance above the confluence. The track then continues alongside the Boyle, joins a farm track inland to a deer fence and follows the fence uphill through manuka and beech forest to meet the Harper Pass Track about 2.5 km west of its Windy Point start. Note that there is not a hut here: the next overnight hut is the slightly dilapidated Hope Shelter 7 km away or the commodious Hope Kiwi Lodge 14 km distant.

As you join the Harper Pass Track, you also join one of New Zealand's most famous fault lines — the 230 km Hope Fault. The last major earthquake here in 1888, ruptured the land along a 40 km stretch of the fault, parallel to the Hope River below you.

canterbury

THE LAND

The Canterbury region is aligned southwest to northeast, and its landscape falls into three parallel strips: the alpine belt, the high-country shoulder, and the plain. Te Araroa's through-route treads two of those strips. The trail crosses the Southern Alps twice on low passes, then heads across the high country east of the alps. The closest it gets to treading the third strip — the plain — is the flat, tussocked expanse of the Mackenzie Basin which, like the Canterbury Plains further north, was formed by glaciers snouting out of mountain valleys, by braided rivers, and by loess-laden winds.

Beech forest gives way to tussock as you tramp the high country and here the landscape speaks as much of what's gone as what's there. You'll pass below Aoraki Mt Cook, the cloud piercer: New Zealand's highest mountain, but the top fell off it 20 years ago, and every day, more minutely, but with just as much finality, single rocks are dislodged from every alpine flank. Everything is falling down here. Millimetre by millimetre since the beginning of its uplift 6.4 million years ago, the Alpine Fault has pushed up 25 km of greywacke and schist: sufficient to finger the stratosphere, yet weather and rocky weakness have turned all but the last 3.5 km of that immense wall into humble scree, outwash gravels, sand, and loess soils by the trillions of tonnes. All of it drifts east, and whenever Te Araroa's route descends off the hills and into the river valleys, it tramps the surfaces of it.

Mesopotamia Station from the Sinclair Range.

THE PEOPLE

The Anglicans who founded Christchurch in the 1850s set in place a civilised enclave from which settlers made their way west, into tough country that would, with passing decades, give them an identity distinct from the gracious founding city in the east.

Explorers and surveyors ventured into alpine fastness, found passes and climbed summits, and the opportunities remain for every kind of difficulty. Mountaineers, wilderness trampers and hunters are still going for it, way beyond the pale.

New Zealand settlers had to raise a productive economy, and in Canterbury they did it on the sheep's back. Runholders ventured on horseback to find their favoured runs then raced — sometimes literally against rival claimants — to the Christchurch Lands Office to register claims. Such were the beginnings of high-country sheep stations that cover 20 per cent of the South Island, the culture of which is as distinct within New Zealand as the West is to America. The stations have their own remembered histories, their family continuity, their personal graveyards, their sheep stringing away on the hills, their sheep dogs, horseback shepherds and their remote musterers' huts. The stations usually run the noble merino. They have huge prestige, and they have their politics. The stations were founded on Crown pastoral leases, and in a new century that offers opportunities beyond pastoral farming for this land, friction has been inevitable with the Crown over rental charges, permissions for alternative use, and access for recreation. In 1998 the Crown set up a framework to divide the stations into public conservation land and freehold farmland. Crown Tenure Review, the voluntary but protracted process that began then, is ongoing still and Te Araroa's route has benefited from it.

THE TRAIL crosses the Southern Alps at Harper Pass (962 m). Low passes through the alps are rare, so it was well used in the past — by Maori as a greenstone route, and by miners going over from Canterbury during the West Coast gold rush in the 1860s.

In 1867 a more direct road route to the coast opened through Arthur's Pass, and the Harper Pass Track lapsed. Yet it has its intrinsic delights — a hot pool, a crossing of the alps — and in the 1930s the Physical Welfare Division of the Department of Internal Affairs built four substantial huts along the route. The department was mindful of the Milford Track's success, but Harper Pass never got those kind of legs. It remains lightly used, but is easy and interesting — easy, that is, except for its length, and for the unbridged crossings of the Taramakau and Otehake rivers at the southern end (and unless you use the flood bridge, the Otira River too). Trampers with river-crossing experience will ford these rivers safely in normal to low flows but when river levels are high, they're impassable. Carry extra food in order to back-track to huts or camp while waiting for river levels to subside.

The track shadows the Hope Fault throughout, a splinter fault that angles east away from the Alpine Fault and eases the strain of New Zealand's contending plates by sideways slippage. After the Hope's magnitude 7.1 quake of 1888, government geologist Alexander McKay poked about here, and is often credited with being the first person to document slip-strike faulting as an effect distinct from vertical rupture. McKay, an eager amateur photographer, posed his son William leaning against a six-wire waratah fence line on the Glenn Wye Station, just a few kilometres east of Windy Point. The photo showed a tussocked sheep paddock apparently little disturbed, but with a fence line offset by the earthquake 2.6 metres. The photo helped convince geologists worldwide of the slip-strike's powerful effect, over time, on landforms.

1. Junction to Hope Kiwi Lodge. Once inside the forest the track sidles above the Hope River for about two hours to Hope Shelter, a six-bunk hut that's old, but useable. The track continues through the forest and then breaks out onto grassy flats, crosses the Hope River on a swing bridge, and at the junction with the St Jacobs Hut track turns left and continues for 2 km to Hope Kiwi Lodge near the forest edge, a good hut, with a fire, firewood rounds, and an axe. (Distance 14 km.)

HARPER PASS TRACK (STAGE 1)

NORTHERN START	Junction with Harper Pass Access
SOUTHERN END	No. 3 Hut
DISTANCE	75 km total. This stage 41 km.
MAPS	92, 93, 94, 95
TRACK STANDARD	Tramping

2. Hope Kiwi Lodge to Hurunui Hut. Beyond the lodge, the track crosses open cattle flats and climbs through bush to Kiwi Saddle (677 m) and a lookout over Lake Sumner. It descends to the lakeshore and a swing bridge over Three Mile Stream. Continue to the lake head and keep going just over 4 km along the flats — the turn towards the Hurunui River comes later than you expect, and when it does, it's a right angle. A swing bridge takes you over the river and a 30-minute climb brings you to the modern Hurunui Hut with wide windows to gaze onto the valley below and with the back country luxury of sleeping platforms and mattresses. (Distance 17 km.)

3. Hurunui Hut to No. 3 Hut. The track descends from the Hurunui Hut through manuka forest to the valley floor. About 3.5 km on, it winds down from a forest path onto river flat, and passes a rock wall wet with overflow. Look up and you'll see beech trees stained orange by sulphur. A short distance beyond, a sign points to the steaming basin on top of the rock wall, and a notice there: *Amoebic meningitis is fatal and caused by water entering nasal passages. Do not immerse head.* This stark warning is in fact standard for any wild pool, and need not deter trampers from an indulgent soak, to neck level, a Te Araroa highlight.

Beyond the hot spring the track continues through flats and forest on the Hurunui's true right all the way to No. 3 Hut. This is one of the original four huts on the route, and remains a comfortable 16-bunk, 1930s wonder. A DOC research building stands nearby. (Distance 10 km.)

ough-tramper Clare Quested on Hurunui swing bridge, Harper Pass Track.

pool, Harper Pass Track.

to Arthur's Pass

Jacksons

73
railway

Mt Alexander 1958

Deception River

Otira River

73

Morrison Footbridge

Taramakau River

Aickens

Crooked River

Lake
Kaurapataka

Otehake River

ARTHUR'S PASS
NATIONAL PARK

KAIMATA RANGE

Kiwi Hut

Harper Pass
Track

Taramakau River

Locke Strm

Locke Stream Hut

M A I N

Harper Pass

DIVIDE

Hurunui River

Harper Pass Bivvy

C R A W F O R D

LAKE SUMNER
FOREST PARK

Cameron Hut

Cameron Strm

Harper Pass
Track

R A N G E

Hurunui No. 3 Hut

Hurunui River (south)

LAKE SUMNER
FOREST PARK

Hurunui River

hot spring

Mackenzie Strm

4. No. 3 Hut to Locke Stream Hut. Soon after leaving No. 3 Hut the track comes up to a three-wire bridge across Cameron Stream. Three-wire bridges are one of New Zealand's back-country pleasures — they have hand wires which may snag your pack as you ease your way onto the single foot wire, and they tilt this way and that underfoot, but they're an effective crossing method, and you'd get wet feet at Cameron Stream otherwise.

The four-bunk Cameron Hut is a further 1.5 km across the flats, then the track leaves cattle country and ascends towards Harper Pass Bivvy, a cramped two-bunk, orange-coloured box with one tiny window and a helpful sign on the inside of the door that reads 'fire exit'.

Some boulder-hopping follows up the steep Hurunui headwaters, and after the dominant beech forest below, it's a pleasure now to see the urchin heads of dracophyllum, the giant buttercup known as the Mt Cook lily, the mountain holly, the tree fuchsia, turpentine shrubs, and mountain pine. At 962 m you breast the Main Divide and sight the Taramakau River winding into the western distance.

In 1857 Kaiapoi Maori told a Pakeha mate, young Edwin Lock, a sawyer and surveyor, of a pass across the Southern Alps and a river beyond leading to the West Coast. Lock mapped the route and, as Lock family history has it, went to claim a £100 prize put up by the Canterbury Provincial Council for anyone who found the way through to the West Coast. A party sent out to test the route included, aside from Lock and four Maori guides, Leonard Harper, son of the first Anglican Bishop of Christchurch. The party confirmed the route, and the pass was named for the bishop's son. What happened to the prize is unknown.

Lock missed getting his name on the pass, but it's perpetuated at the misspelled Locke Stream, and Locke Stream Hut is now 5 km away, on a track that drops 450 m in altitude. Immediately beyond the pass it descends steeply on gravels where it's easy to skid — this was accident alley when the pack-horses were brought across the pass in the old days. The track then splashes across the upper Taramakau River before crossing the river again on a swing bridge, to the true left.

As the track begins to level off, the native nettle ongaonga has colonised its margins, and fossicking kiwi often leave their large, three-pronged foot prints on patches of soft ground around here. Any long whistle in the night is also likely to be kiwi.

HARPER PASS TRACK (STAGE 2)

NORTHERN START	No. 3 Hut
SOUTHERN END	Morrison Footbridge
DISTANCE	75 km total. This stage 34 km.
MAPS	95, 96, 97
TRACK STANDARD	Tramping

Locke Stream Hut is another original, built by 65-year-old packman Sam Burrows in 1940, with hand-hewn timber transported to the site by horse and sledge. The hut was restored in 1993 through a bequest from the Tom Beeston estate. It has a radio link to DOC's Arthur's Pass National Park Visitor Centre and you can request weather forecasts from there. (Distance 14 km.)

5. Locke Stream Hut to Morrison Footbridge. The tramp downriver from Locke Stream Hut is through unmarked bush and open river terraces, but with frequent crossings and re-crossings of the Taramakau River. They're not a problem in normal summer flows, but impossible after heavy rain, and Kiwi Hut, located about halfway down the route, is a refuge if necessary. Onward from there, it's safest to approach the Otehake River from the true left of the Taramakau, and to cross it separately. It's a tributary to the larger Taramakau, but its single u-shaped bed makes it a more challenging crossing than its bigger, braided brother.

Beyond the Otehake, the route stays on the Taramakau's true left down to the signposted turnoff onto the flood track, and a final two hours of sharp climbs and descents along a steep face above the Otira River to the Morrison Footbridge across the Otira. Cross the footbridge to access State Highway 73. (Distance 20 km.)

If you want to resupply, turn left on State Highway 73 to Arthur's Pass Village, 19 km distant. Buses serve this route, or you can hitchhike. The township has everything needed for resupply, and DOC's Visitor Centre is located here.
Note: Trampers wishing to finish the track more quickly can exit onto the Aickens car park on State Highway 73 by continuing down the Taramakau past the flood-track turnoff and past the shelter. If you do this you must be prepared to ford the Otira River, which is dangerous after rain.

ough-tramper Clare Quested fords the upper Hurunui River toward Harper Bivvy.

THE MOUNTAIN-RUN LEG of the celebrated Coast to Coast multisport event goes up the Deception River, over Goat Pass (1070 m), and down the Mingha River and river valley. Top athletes complete the run in around three hours; most trampers will take one or two days.

The track bounces from side to side of both rivers, particularly the Deception, where there's at least 10 significant crossings in the lower river, and more in the upper reaches, where flows are lighter. The crossings militate against attempting any tramp in heavy rain or when heavy rain is forecast.

NORTHERN START	State Highway 73 at Morrisons Footbridge
SOUTHERN END	State Highway 73 at Greyneys Shelter
DISTANCE	24 km
MAPS	97, 98
TRACK STANDARD	Hard tramping

1. State Highway 73 to Goat Pass Hut. Cross the Otira River on the Morrison Footbridge and follow the track across river flats on the true right of the Deception River. Cross to the true left and follow rock cairns through the lower gorge, crossing the river as necessary. The tracks either side of the river are sometimes marked, sometimes not.

Five and a half kilometres upriver you may smell the sulphurous Midday Creek. Stay alert for a reputed hot pool in a flood channel a few hundred metres on from here. It's elusive, and may be washed out to little more than a spring, and if you bathe, don't put your head under. Upper Deception Hut, 7 km further upriver on a bushy terrace on the true right, is similarly hard to spot.

Beyond this hut, the river pours and pools through boulders and you can clamber forward on smooth grey stone. As the Deception bends left 13.5 km into the tramp, follow straight ahead up a rocky channel to Goat Pass Hut. The hut has a radio link for weather information and a veranda to just sit on and look at the view. The mountaintops are everywhere. (Distance 14 km.)

2. Goat Pass Hut to Greyneys Shelter. The track is boardwalked south of the hut and meets the Mingha River 1.5 km on. It goes past the Mingha Bivvy, and 5 km on from the pass, sidesteps a deep river gorge at Dudley's Knob. It rejoins the Mingha again on flats where the channel wanders, and you'll cross and re-cross until this river meets the Bealey. Look for a safe crossing of the Bealey River above this confluence to reach State Highway 73 and Greyneys Shelter. (Distance 11 km.)

If you need to resupply, you can walk or hitchhike 5 km back to Arthur's Pass. The campsite at Greyneys Shelter is free and has toilets and water from a stream.

KLONDYKE TRACK

NORTHERN START	State Highway 73 at Greyneys Shelter
SOUTHERN END	Cora Lynn car park
DISTANCE	7.5 km
MAPS	98, 99
TRACK STANDARD	Tramping

THIS TRACK WILL INTEREST mainly Te Araroa through-walkers. The riverbed becomes the trail. From Greyneys Shelter follow the riverbed down to Klondyke Corner campsite, then follow the true right gravel of the Bealey from Klondyke Corner to ford the Waimakariri River, just in front of the Bealey Hotel.

The Bealey Hotel has backpacker and motel accommodation, a restaurant and bar. Walk 4 km up State Highway 73 to Cora Lynn Rd and through the gate marked Cass Lagoon Track to the car park. The six-bunk Bealey Hut is a short distance up the track.

HARPER RIVER TRACK (STAGE 1)

NORTHERN START	Cora Lynn car park
SOUTHERN END	Hamilton Hut
DISTANCE	33 km total. This stage 14 km.
MAPS	98, 99
TRACK STANDARD	Tramping

THE TRACK CLIMBS THROUGH forest to cross the broad north face of Mt Bruce on tussock country high above the wide braided shingle of the Waimakariri. From Lagoon Saddle the soggiest sections of track are boardwalked down to the bushline, then the track descends past the two-bunk Lagoon Saddle Shelter to the Harper River and river crossings that are usually straightforward. Nine kilometres in, you'll pass West Harper Hut, whose axe-hewn beams, dirt floor and canvas bunks are a reminder of the old back country huts.

Five kilometres on from there, across a swing bridge and a three-wire bridge, you'll find a hut that boldly presents the new. Its wide riverstone fireplace, its subdued outlook across river terraces, its screens, drying wires, and general space have earned Hamilton Hut the nickname Hamilton Hilton. It was built in the early 1980s, in the days when the Craigieburn Forest Park had an advisory board of keen trampers, and a sympathetic Conservator of Forests could pony up the funds and the architects to make a hut to dream on. It has a radio link through to the Arthur's Pass Visitor Centre.

roup of adventure runners test the Deception River route led by Chris Cox (without shirt).

milton Hut, Harper River Track.

RETURN TO THE SIGN at the true left side of Hamilton Creek. The track then continues around to the Harper River confluence and continues downriver. An old four-wheel-drive track makes easy tramping, but there's a number of river crossings and, with that in mind, you'll need to judge the river flow. Eight kilometres downriver, the Pinnacles stand on the true right like a miniature of Antoni Gaudi's *Sagrada Familia* cathedral — erosion has sculpted the compacted sand and gravel outcrop into a striking series of spires, with pebble caps. You can find marine fossils in nearby rocks.

If the river is high it's possible to remain on the true left all the way down to the Pinnacles without too much additional effort or time. TAT is seeking a way to remain on the true left all the way through to Harper Rd and make this an all-weather route. Currently, though, you'll need to cross often, with a final crossing to the Harper's true right just before the confluence with the Avoca River. Cross the Avoca separately then follow the farm track on the Harper's true right, and bear left across the Harper River bridge. Four hundred metres beyond the bridge, Harper Rd turns off left.

TrustPower has a free overnight campsite available a further 400 m from the Harper Village road junction, down the unnamed road with the '2 km to Lake Coleridge' sign. The campsite is signposted on the left and the toilet is further down towards the lake on the Oakden Canal. Walk down Harper Rd to Homestead Rd. Turn right onto Homestead Rd and after 1 km watch for the start of Lake Hill Track.

HARPER RIVER TRACK (STAGE 2)

NORTHERN START	Hamilton Hut
SOUTHERN END	Harper Rd
DISTANCE	33 km total. This stage 19 km.
MAPS	99, 100
TRACK STANDARD	Tramping

LAKE HILL TRACK follows a narrow strip of unformed legal road. From the stile, the track crosses farmland where stock may be grazing, then crosses a swamp fringe which may be wet underfoot. Resist the temptation to follow the farm track around: property owners want you to keep to the track.

Beyond the wetland, the track follows a four-wheel-drive farm track then diverges left to the Lake Coleridge shoreline, climbs a bluff then descends to lake level again. The boardwalk at the foot of the cliffs here is sometimes a few centimetres underwater, but only during maximum lake-storage levels.

LAKE HILL TRACK

NORTHERN START	Homestead Rd
SOUTHERN END	Coleridge Intake Rd
DISTANCE	3 km
MAPS	101
TRACK STANDARD	Tramping

The track away from the lake is well marked, sometimes joining and sometimes departing from the farm track. Follow the markers and they'll lead you across a stile to Coleridge Intake Rd.

Walkers wishing to use the track simply to access Lake Coleridge can avoid the wetland section by coming in from this end, 1.5 km down Coleridge Intake Rd from the Algidus Rd intersection.

Walk up Coleridge Intake Rd and across the Algidus Rd intersection to the entrance to TrustPower land, marked by a cattle stop.

ARBORETUM TRACK

NORTHERN START	Coleridge Intake Rd stock gate
SOUTHERN END	Hummocks Rd, Lake Coleridge Village
DISTANCE	1.6 km
MAPS	101
TRACK STANDARD	Tramping

CROSS THE CATTLE STOP AND follow the Coleridge Intake Rd in. Turn right onto the off-road track just as the road makes a hairpin turn left. This leads to the Lake Coleridge power station's penstocks. Follow these pipes down a short distance, then turn left into pine forest and through open country to a gate. Here the track enters a 2 hectare arboretum established by Harry Hart, superintendent of the power station for 30 years through to 1954, who planted out one of New Zealand's best conifer collections. Follow the arboretum path through to a memorial gate and an exit on Hummocks Rd, Lake Coleridge Village.

The nearby Lake Coleridge Lodge offers dinner, bed and breakfast. You're now on the banks of the Rakaia River, a large braided river with an unsettled shingle bed. Even in low flows it's not possible to safely ford this river near Te Araroa trailheads on either bank. The riverbed does not form part of Te Araroa. This is a Hazard Zone, and you should not risk a foot crossing in any circumstances. When you arrive at the lodge, the owners will assist in identifying transport options through to the Clent Hills trailhead on the south bank of the Rakaia.

w across Lake Coleridge from Lake Hill Track.

e first government-owned power station in New Zealand at Lake Coleridge, Arboretum Track.

Harpers Knob

Hakatere–Potts Rd

bridge

Lake
Clearwater

Lake Camp

Lake Clearwater

Potts River

Lake Emma

Mt Guy

DOGS RANGE

Clearwater Track

Dogs Hill

Ashburton River (south)

Hakatere

to Mt Somers village

Buicks Bridge

Maori Lakes

Castleridge Station

car park

Hakatere–Heron Rd

Lake
Heron

Lake Emily

Emily Hill

Manuka Lake

Seagull Lake

Swin River

Manuka Hut

Swin River (south)

Mt Sugarloaf 1238

Mt Taylor 2333

Double Hut

Mellish Strm

TAYLOR RANGE

Swin River (north)

Clent Hills Track

Smite River

Clent Hills Saddle

HAKATERE
CONSERVATION
PARK

Round Hill Ck

Godley Peak 208

Ashburton River (north)

Comyns Hut

Mutton Gully

Turtons Strm

Clent Hills Track

A-frame Hut

Turtons Saddle

BLACK HILL RANGE

Glenrock Strm

Double Hill Run Rd

Rakaia River

N

THIRTY-SEVEN KILOMETRES up from State Highway 77, when Blackford Rd has turned to Double Hill Run Rd, and dwindled to fords across the side streams, a DOC sign at Glenrock Stream signals the Clent Hills Track. Trampers should be well-equipped, with map-reading and back-country skills.

NORTHERN START	Glenrock Stream
SOUTHERN END	Hakatere Heron Rd
DISTANCE	46 km
MAPS	102, 103, 104
TRACK STANDARD	Hard tramping

1. Track Entrance to Comyns Hut. Follow the stream up past a kowhai grove. Five kilometres into the tramp you'll cross into the Hakatere Conservation Park and begin a steep climb up an old farm track, 1.5 km to Turtons Saddle (1120 m).

The farm track comes around the left side of the Turtons Stream catchment, and descends to the tidy little A-frame, three-bunk hut. The track follows Turtons Stream for the next 4.5 km, crossing as necessary, but is back on the true left side to negotiate Mutton Gully, and fords Turtons Stream one last time to a river terrace where the original 1890s Comyns Hut stands derelict. The newer eight-bunk Comyns Hut, built in 1957, is alongside. The door and walls of the newer hut are an informal record of past musterers, listed always in order of seniority with the packie — the man who brought in the musterers' gear by pack-horse — falling in at the rear. Also on these walls, hunters record their bags of deer and chamois.

The Clent Hills Station dates back to 1857 as a 20,000 hectare run under licence from the Crown, but by the early 1920s rabbits had eaten out its grazing lands. The Buick family picked up the lease in 1923 and spent three years eradicating the rabbits before restocking.

In 2004 the Nature Heritage Fund bought most of the station's high-country hills to add onto the Hakatere Conservation Park, and the station itself is now a 2000 hectare rump within the Heron Basin. (Distance 14 km.)

2. Comyns Hut to Double Hut. This section is challenging and crosses exposed high-country terrain. DOC estimates it's a six- to eight-hour tramp, with no hut along the way, though it's all conservation parkland and you can camp anywhere.

A marker behind the hut points west up the North Branch of the Ashburton River and on up Round Hill Creek. Travel is confined within these watercourses, with frequent crossings, but is straightforward in normal flows. Trampers will pick their own route through matagouri and rough terrain, between marker poles that won't be readily visible in poor weather. Five and a half kilometres in, the track departs the creek to climb through thick tussock to Clent Hills Saddle (1480 m) with wide views across the Heron Basin 800 m below.

Take care with the route beyond the saddle, as there's a gap in the marker poles. Don't descend: continue to the right along the saddle and link to the uppermost animal track, cross the large scree slope, then sidle on through tussock towards the next ridge. Marker poles show up again, and lead you down to a stream crossing, a short climb to the Mellish Saddle, then over and down to the Heron Basin. You'll pass a signposted junction through to Lake Heron, but continue left and cross the North Branch of the Swin River to a second junction. Turn left here on 1 km side track to arrive at Double Hut. (Distance 17 km.)

3. Double Hut to Lake Emily car park. The track continues south, crossing the Swin River South Branch, and on for 6.5 km through a landscape of gravel flats and rippling moraine ridges from the long-ago glaciation here. It passes Seagull and Manuka lakes to a junction where a side track leads upstream to Manuka Hut. The stream's water is potable.

Continuing straight on over flats for 2 km, the route then climbs over a low ridge on Emily Hill and sidles down to a car park at Lake Emily. It leaves the Hakatere Conservation Park here to join a marked paper road across Castleridge Station. Trampers should follow the markers carefully to avoid straying onto private property.

About 600 metres from the track exit is a farm gate that should be left open or closed as found. (Distance 14 km.)

Turn left onto Hakatere Heron Rd and walk through to the Hakatere Track trailhead at Buicks Bridge. If you need to hitch hike to town for resupply, continue on the road 3.5 km beyond Buicks Bridge, then turn left at the T-junction 23 km along Ashburton Gorge Rd to Mt Somers Village.

…aia River from the Clent Hills Track.

…ough-tramper 'Clod', Clent Hills Track.

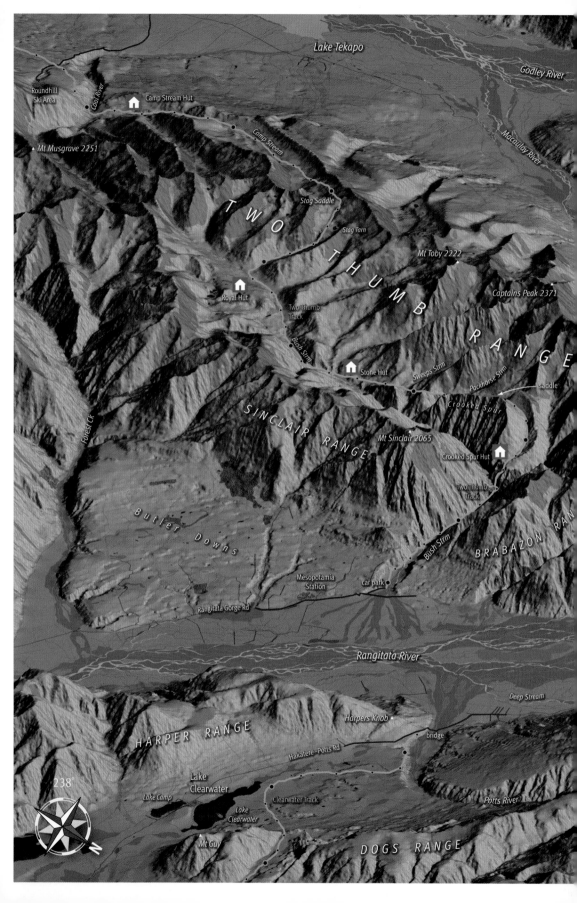

MARKER POLES LEAD WEST from the south side of Buicks Bridge towards the gap between Dogs Hill and Mt Guy. (See map on page 208 for track start.) During the last ice age, an ice lobe from the Rangitata Glacier covered the Clearwater Basin, advancing and retreating until it melted out 12,000 years ago. The sediments of that incursion remain mostly undisturbed and they now upholster the basin in pleasingly rounded forms.

The first 5 km of the walk is an intrusion into the silence and power of these unmodified remnants. Then you hit civilisation — a fence — then an old farm track for 5 km. The track rises gradually to a saddle on the same slopes where the 200 m face of the ice sheet once creaked through, coming the other way. The outlook south from the saddle is memorable: the basin stretches away to the great dusty incision made by the Rangitata, with the perpetual snows of the alps standing behind.

The track heads over moraines and meltwater channels towards Lake Clearwater, and as you pass beyond the tip of the lake you'll see kettleholes, the odd erratic rock, and the kame terraces on Harpers Knob — the sculpted platforms left by the ice lobe that once shouldered its way into this basin.

From the left-hand lip of the Potts River, the track follows the fence line, then drops down a gully to the river. If the river is running clear the best travel is downstream to the Potts River car park at the road bridge. If the river is discoloured this route is unwise, and trampers should go up the other side of the gully and remain inside the fence line through to the road. From here it's a short walk downhill to the car park.

The Rangitata is a large braided river with an unsettled shingle bed. It poses a significant danger to trampers on foot. The riverbed does not form part of Te Araroa. This is a Hazard Zone and TAT does not recommend a crossing on foot.

The Potts River and Bush Stream trailheads on either side of the Rangitata make ideal beginning or end points for Te Araroa section trampers. Through-trampers are the only people needing to connect the trailheads on the north and south sides of the river. They should consult TAT's website for up-to-date details of transport options. Fit adults with river-crossing experience can cross the Rangitata in low-flow late summer conditions. The cross-point is above the confluence with the Potts River, and the first channel — Deep Stream — gives an early indication of the flows.

CLEARWATER TRACK

NORTHERN START	Buicks Bridge, Hakatere Heron Rd
SOUTHERN END	Potts River Bridge car park
DISTANCE	21 km
MAPS	104, 105, 106
TRACK STANDARD	Tramping

TWO THUMB TRACK (STAGE 1)

NORTHERN START	Bush Stream car park
SOUTHERN END	Lilybank Rd
DISTANCE	57 km total. This stage 19 km.
MAPS	106, 107
TRACK STANDARD	Hard tramping

THE TRAILHEAD FOR THIS challenging high-country track is within Mesopotamia Station. The Prouting family has managed the station since 1945 — the latest chapter of a distinguished history.

The station was founded in 1860 by Samuel Butler, an ardent Darwinian, opportunist sheep farmer, and author of the famous *Erewhon*, a satirical novel about a lost civilisation in country not unlike Mesopotamia Station itself. The attention to science during Mesopotamia's first year had a tragic end when the Colonial Secretary Andrew Sinclair returned downriver from an expedition with Julius von Haast, the Canterbury geologist, in March 1861 and drowned in the Rangitata. His grave is at the riverside.

1. Bush Stream car park to Crooked Spur Hut. Follow markers from the car park up towards Bush Stream, then use the streambed or adjacent bank. The crossings are straightforward in normal flows but tricky after rain or during the snowmelt of spring. Cross Bush Stream for a final time at a concrete slab, the last remains of an old swing bridge, and climb from the true left side on a formed pack track to the five-bunk Crooked Spur Hut, used up until 2009 for mustering. (Distance 10 km.)

2. Crooked Spur Hut to Stone Hut. The unformed track goes behind Crooked Spur, climbs steadily to a saddle at 1500 m, then descends across Pack Horse and Sweeps streams and returns to Bush Stream. Follow the true left bank to an old stock bridge and cross it to the eight-bunk Stone Hut, which has a bath and long-drop toilet nearby. (Distance 9 km.)

Looking towards Harpers Knob, Clearwater Track.

Trampers on Mt Sinclair above Two Thumb Track.

3. Stone Hut to Royal Hut. Follow along the true right of Bush Stream to the eight-bunk Royal Hut. (See map on page 212 for track start.) In March 1970 three RNZAF Iroquois helicopters descended onto the flats beside what was then called Tin Hut and debouched the Cliff Rescue Squad, the Diplomatic Protection Squad and a young prince and princess: Charles, then aged 21, and Anne, then aged 19. The two had accompanied their mother Queen Elizabeth II to New Zealand for the Captain Cook bicentennial celebrations, had laid up out of the public eye at Mt Peel Station awhile, then been choppered up for a look at the musterers' top beat on Mesopotamia.

There was at this time an open fire. There was billy tea. There was an alpine gecko that appeared from nowhere outside the hut and disappeared again and was hunted by the hands of a princess, who turned over a lot of rocks. Then the royal party left as suddenly as it had arrived, and Tin Hut was renamed Royal Hut thereafter. (Distance 6 km.)

4. Royal Hut to Camp Stream Hut. From Royal Hut, the poled route leads away through tussock to a 5 km climb, steep in places but safe enough in reasonable weather, to pass Stag Tarn, and reach Stag Saddle (1925 m). This is Te Araroa's highest point, and if the weather's clear you'll see Lake Tekapo. Rock flour, ground by glaciers in the alpine catchments, turns the lake an otherworldly teal blue. This is the first and at 700 m altitude, the highest of the Mackenzie Basin's big alpine lakes.

There's cellphone coverage here, and one other thing — if you can see Tekapo, Tekapo can see you, and so can the observatory on Mt John. The observatory site was chosen for the clarity and darkness of this central South Island spot, and the starlight. On Stag Saddle you've just set foot on the northeastern edge of a protective Dark Skies Zone that runs south from here all the way through the Mackenzie District, beyond Lake Tekapo to Lake Pukaki and almost to Twizel. It's the only extended Dark Skies Zone in New Zealand, and within it, all outdoor lights must be shielded downwards, and all blue or ultraviolet wavelengths screened out. From the saddle, in good weather the descent can be made down the ridge on the right hand side — affording excellent views across Lake Tekapo to Mt Cook. However in foul weather, or those less confident navigating, it is recommended to follow the well-marked route down into Camp Stream Valley.

NORTHERN START	Stone Hut
SOUTHERN END	Lilybank Rd
DISTANCE	57 km total. This stage 38 km.
MAPS	107, 108, 109, 110
TRACK STANDARD	Tramping

The track is poled down into Camp Stream Valley, though at times the markers can be hard to find, and this final crossing onto the western side of the Two Thumb Range demands a careful descent in cloud or fog. Eight kilometres after it reaches the valley floor, it joins a four-wheel-drive track close to the eroded edge of Camp Stream and follows that track to the six-bunk Camp Stream Hut. It's a tin hut, old, small, and brown with rust, but in good condition, with a corrugated-iron water tank upturned alongside, just for the dog. (Distance 14.5 km.)

5. Camp Stream Hut to Boundary Stream car park.
Coal River is 2 km past the hut, steep-sided and dense with matagouri. It's a short climb down one side and up the other, and a brief tramp through high tussock to the ski field road. For trampers who're using the Two Thumb route as a stand-alone tramp and want to exit, it's 6.5 km down this access to a car park on Lilybank Rd. Te Araroa's route continues straight ahead, across the ski field road and along the base of the Two Thumb Range. This final 13 km crosses Washdyke Stream to reach Boundary Stream, then follows it down on the true right bank to a second car park further south on Lilybank Rd. (Distance 17 km.)

Walk down Lilybank Rd to the Lake Tekapo Regional Park, which offers a final 2 km lakeside walk into Tekapo village. The lakeside track passes Tekapo's two most famous structures: the squat riverstone glory of the Church of the Good Shepherd, and the solid bronze sheep-dog statue. Its Gaelic inscription — Brannachdan air na cu caurach — is a nod to the Scots, and the district's debt to the sheep dog is recognised in English also — 'without the help of which the grazing of this mountainous country would be impossible'. Onward from there, Lake Tekapo village has a shopping centre sufficient to most needs, including a motor camp and a Four Square store for resupply.

rough-tramper Lucy Cant mugs above Godley Valley, Two Thumb Track.

urch of the Good Shepherd, Lake Tekapo.

THE MACKENZIE BASIN is a world apart, a flatland isolated by mountains, once glaciated by ice, then aggregated by rivers, and finally reticulated by engineers. Two things have interested the engineers: the basin gathers a vast runoff from the alps, and it also slopes very gently south, with descending lakes. Lake Tekapo and all the Mackenzie Basin lakes south of it have been dammed, their waters piped down to hydro-electricity turbines, and canals built to carry the water onward to the next turbines.

From Lake Tekapo township, follow Te Araroa finger signs up Aorangi Crescent into Andrew Don Drive, to Scott Pond. A stile leads over the security fence. Tekapo A Power Station stands off to your right as you cross a control gate and head down the canal. Stay on the true left of the canal.

1. Tekapo A Power Station to Lake Pukaki. Follow along the canal's true left for 12 km to State Highway 8, crossing the highway with care. As you return to the canal, Irishman Creek Station, once home to Bill Hamilton (inventor of the jet boat), adjoins the opposite side of the canal. Hamilton tested his prototype on the dam and water race near here before proving its revolutionary potential on the Waitaki River in 1954.

TEKAPO– TWIZEL TRACK

NORTHERN START	Lake Tekapo village
SOUTHERN END	Twizel
DISTANCE	54 km
MAPS	110, 111, 112, 113, 114
TRACK STANDARD	Easy tramping

Tekapo Canal.

On a clear day the summit ridge of New Zealand's highest mountain, Aoraki Mt Cook (3764 m), juts above the high country out to the right. The track passes a sockeye salmon farm immersed in the canal, then past a popular fishing spot where anglers jostle for an easy catch. At the end of the canal, the route continues straight down the hill to meet Lake Pukaki. (Distance 28 km.)

2. Lake Pukaki to Pines Camp. The track then follows the Lake Pukaki shoreline alongside Hayman Rd for 7 km, following the Alps to Ocean cycleway as it weaves on and off the road and formed lakeside route initially, then stays off-road on well-formed track all the way to Pines Camp. Aoraki Mt Cook rises beyond the Pukaki lake head, and whether by roiling cloud on its shoulders or by sunlit angle on its crisp summit facets it changes with every

Aoraki Mt Cook from Lake Pukaki, Tekapo-Twizel Track.

passing minute. Pines Camp is not a formal campground but has two long-drop toilets.

One kilometre on across the Pukaki High Dam, what was once an information centre has toilets and a water fountain, but is not a campsite. (Distance 12 km.)

3. Pines Camp to Twizel. Walk the dam and continue along State Highway 8 to turn left off the highway just before the visitor centre, where the Alps to Ocean cycleway continues across the Pukaki Flats. It is pleasant walking, but be warned it can be very exposed in hot or poor weather.

The track passes through Bendrose Reserve and turns left onto a track alongside State Highway 8 into Twizel. Te Araroa finger signs indicate the crossing point across the highway to the town. (Distance 12 km.)

Birchwood Rd

Ahuriri River

Ahuriri Riv

Snowy Gorge Ck

▲ *Snowy Peak 1845*

DIADEM RANGE

East Ahuriri Track

Ahuriri River (east)

old shearers' hut

Ohau Peak 1917

East Ahuriri Track

OHAU RANGE

▲ Pt 1489

Pt 151

Quailburn Station

OHAU MORAINES

WETLANDS COMPLEX

Freehold Ck

Sawyers

historic provincial boundary

Lake Middleton

Lake Ohau Alpine Village

Glen Mar Ski Club

locked gate

Lake Ohau

Ohau Track

Maori Swamp

Ben Ohau 1522

Lake Ohau Rd

BEN OHAU RANGE

weir

Table Hill

Ohau Track

Ohau River

Ohau Canal

8

Wairepo Arm

Lake Ruataniwha

TWIZEL

Ruataniwha Dam
Ohau B Canal

Bendrose Reserve

Twizel River

241°

8

Tekapo – Twizel Track

Pukaki Canal

Twizel River

EXIT TWIZEL ON Ruataniwha Rd to State Highway 8, and follow the metalled walk/cycleway south for 2 km to cross the spillway, then the bridge over the Ohau B Canal. Once over the bridge and before reaching the salmon farm, cross the highway onto a terrace track beside Lake Ruataniwha. The lake is the smallest of the Mackenzie Basin hydro lakes, a last collection bucket for Tekapo and Pukaki and Ohau lake water before it flows down to Lake Benmore and the dams east. It's a recreational lake, and a great rowing venue.

After 3 km the terrace track links to a rough riverside road, and from here to Lake Ohau, the tramp is on- or off-road as tracks permit, 12 km through to a weir, then head west to Lake Ohau's shoreline. Four kilometres on, stock tracks close to the shoreline take you past Maori Swamp. Along the track ahead you'll climb four fences through to a locked gate just before Lake Ohau Rd. Here you cross the old 1861 spade-line boundary between Otago and Canterbury. The two provincial governments were each issuing their own grazing licences over the same land and abusing each other over this before central government finally stepped in to insist on a visible boundary. The ditch boundary disregarded local geography, however, and lapsed 38 years later. One kilometre up the road, to the left, there's an historic site where the ditch is still visible.

From the locked gate a short road section brings you through to the Lake Middleton shoreline. Walk east around the lake to the campground at its head. If you don't plan to camp here, go on another 2.5 km on the road shoulder past the Alpine Village then onto a good track along the Ohau lakefront to the Glen Mary Ski Club.

OHAU TRACK

NORTHERN START	Ruataniwha Rd-State Highway 8 junction
SOUTHERN END	Glen Mary Ski Club
DISTANCE	33 km
MAPS	114, 115, 116
TRACK STANDARD	Tramping

EAST AHURIRI TRACK

NORTHERN START	Glen Mary Ski Club
SOUTHERN END	Birchwood Road
DISTANCE	24 km
MAPS	116, 117
TRACK STANDARD	Tramping

FOLLOW THE FOUR-WHEEL-DRIVE TRACK uphill from Glen Mary Ski Club to join the mountain-bike track which traverses to Sawyers Creek then Freehold Creek. DOC markers lead up beside the creek through beech forest to pass an informal campsite just below the treeline.

From the treeline, Te Araroa's track initially follows poles and a light ground track on the true left of Freehold Creek towards Dumbbell Lake, then departs the marked route and traverses over to the East Ahuriri River valley. This traverse does have markers, but they're sporadic and not always visible one to the next. Navigate between Pts 1489 and 1516, favouring the Pt 1516 side to avoid swamps and later bluffs.

The route descends to the East Ahuriri headwaters and down a final crumbling flank into the valley. From here, it's easier travel 5 km downriver and past an old shearers' hut on the true left river terrace. Any tramper seeking better shelter or a more extended halfway stop can continue on a further 1 km, then head out over the saddle that becomes obvious on the left. Another 4.5 km over that saddle and down the gulch beyond, the old Quailburn woolshed has an informal campsite alongside, and a toilet. It's a lengthy diversion though.

Eight kilometres on from the old shearers' hut, the track emerges into the wider Ahuriri River valley and follows along the fence line to the right of the pine trees another 2 km to the riverbank. The Ahuriri can be forded in normal river flows, but it's the largest unbridged flow along Te Araroa's South Island route, so assess it carefully. If you cross here, the track continues almost straight across, on the far bank. If you're unsure about crossing the river, the road bridge 5 km downstream is a bailout option.

Once across the river, trampers walk over to Birchwood Rd along a marked fishing access track, to a car park across the road.

From the car park it's 13 km down Birchwood Rd, and a further 18 km left down State Highway 8 to Omarama if you want to resupply.

apo Canal.

ough-trampers Simon Cook and Nicky Gibson after Maori Swamp heading west on Ohau Track.

otago

THE LAND

Otago is a landscape of great power. The old peneplain, as grooved now as a cortex. The föhn wind. The lenticular billow cloud, should you be lucky enough to see this vast white wind-sculpted masterpiece. The tors, the tussock, the schist, and the gold. The smooth brown hills cast shadows that don't lengthen so much as pool. The Clutha River is singular river royalty, capturing most other Otago rivers on its way through from Lake Wanaka to the coast. And if the alps diminish here, still they cast up one last wonder, the classic alpine horn of Mt Aspiring.

The major fault line that issues out of the Cardrona Valley across the Wanaka Basin and along the bed of Lake Hawea divides Otago into its deeply dissected alpine belt, and the smoother basin and range country to the east. Te Araroa treads one side of that Cardrona Fault, then the other, but whatever side, it moves within a rain shadow. The clag that streams from every alpine valley is reduced here to flickers of lightning and dry thunder. By the time the westerly weather arrives the alps have stripped out its wet skies in favour of a black Otago night with stars or a blue Otago day with sun. Otago is as close as New Zealand gets to a continental mass with a continental climate: hot and dry in summer, and cold enough in winter to crack stone.

Ahuriri Valley from Ben Avon.

THE PEOPLE

They came from Scotland in the 1850s. They were from the Free Church of Scotland and Otago became their field of enterprise. They founded Dunedin on the coast, supported graziers in the hinterland, and worked with wool until the gold rushes of the 1860s turned Dunedin for a time into New Zealand's largest town. Calvinist dedication and skills converted the opportunistic wealth of the gold into institutional permanence and helped found a great ethnic success story that spread out from Otago and continues today. Something close to 20 per cent of New Zealanders have Scottish roots.

Otago has produced a bonnie disproportion of New Zealand's most influential poets, painters, photographers, novelists, arts patrons and also, in last century's Dunedin-edited literary magazine *Landfall*, its most lacerating criticisms of New Zealand life. A clan culture happened to settle a barren landscape, put up a statue of Robbie Burns in the Octagon, and spread the Scottish poet's values of 'Sense and Worth o'er all the earth'. It spread the Scots' tenacious loyalty to the home turf, however barren, and took the fight to any who'd impose on it. The poets et al fight on. It was they who, just a few years back, roundly saw off a plan by a state-owned enterprise to bring wind turbines onto the Lammermoors, one of Otago's outstanding block mountains.

Te Araroa treads mainly the pastoral country of Otago's interiors but sometimes passes stony terraces of pinot gris and pinot noir, classic wine grapes growing in improbably southern latitudes. Too, adventure tourism swings from the bungy bridges, the harnesses of the paragliders, and the broadside spray and wallow of the jet boats. Such managed thrills thrive mostly around Queenstown, the final paradigm of small-town beauty.

Lake Hawea

Pakituhi Hut

Gladstone Reserve
Timaru Creek Rd

foul-weather route

Breast Hill 1578

Corner Peak 1683

Dingle Peak 1835

Breast Hill
Track

Timaru River

take left fork
up hill

Stodys Hut

Little Breast Hill 1638

Breast Hill
Track

Maungatika 1851

Timaru River

Mt Prospect 1770

Top Timaru Hut

Lindis River

Mt Melina 1925

Mt Martha 1906

Mt Martha
Saddle

Breast Hill
Track

Avon Burn

Birchwood Rd

Birchwood Rd to Omarama

Ahuriri River

Ahuriri River

Snowy Peak 1845

234°

Ahuriri River (east)

East Ahuriri
Track

N

THE TRACK ENTERS at Longslip Station, and ends across Lake Hawea Station. Longslip was established in 1858, but was overrun by rabbits and abandoned in 1895. Lake Hawea Station was divided off soon after and since 1912 has been run by the well-known Rowley family. Longslip and Lake Hawea stations entered the Crown Tenure Review (CTR) process in 2002 and 2005 respectively — the leaseholders aiming to freehold, and the Crown to enhance the boundaries of the Ahuriri Conservation Park, where rare black stilts pick their way along river flats, and the Hawea Conservation Park further west, where the New Zealand falcon hunts. Breast Hill (1578 m) lay outside the park zone, and had few champions, but TAT had already scouted a fine entry onto Otago over it, and asked CTR negotiators to include a track line in the public land portion over Breast Hill.

BREAST HILL TRACK

NORTHERN START	Birchwood Rd
SOUTHERN END	Gladstone Reserve
DISTANCE	54 km
MAPS	117, 118, 119, 120
TRACK STANDARD	Tramping

1. Birchwood car park to Top Timaru Hut. A marked route leads off from the car park and follows a fence line towards the Avon Burn. Ford the burn, then climb to a pedestrian gate and join the farm track above the burn's true right bank. Head upstream on the farm track to Mt Martha Saddle (1680 m). Be aware: the approach to the saddle is an avalanche path in winter and spring.

Beyond the saddle, Te Araroa descends on an unmarked bulldozer track then a tussocked track that can wash out as it crosses the side streams to Timaru Creek, but stay on the true left and the four-bunk Top Timaru Hut will appear. (Distance 23 km.)

2. Top Timaru Hut to Stodys Hut. Return to the bulldozed track and continue downstream to the treeline. Progress through the forest is slow on a marked track that climbs, descends and sidles along the true left of this steep-sided river valley, through to a grassy area 2.5 km downstream. From here, you're corralled into a narrow 7 km stretch with a dozen river crossings, straightforward in normal flows, and emerge at the Breast Hill Track–Timaru River Track junction. The track from the junction climbs steeply to the treeline then sidles across tussock country, returns briefly to the forest and reaches the six-bunk Stodys Hut right on the treeline. This old musterers' hut was restored to reasonable condition in 2010 while retaining much of its character. Water is available from the nearby creek — the last reliable water until Pakituhi Hut. (Distance 14.5 km.)

3. Stodys Hut to Pakituhi Hut via Breast Hill. The track's final 16 km, won during CTR, is a Te Araroa highlight. The route leads along a high and broad ridge on an old farm track but its junctions are signposted, there's little navigation to trouble you, and soon the distinctive peak of Mt Aspiring appears as a celestial companion in the west. This is a working farm, and as the ridge rolls on, you may also see the high-altitude merino huddles the musterers call sheep camps.

A foul-weather route departs Te Araroa to the left about 1 km before it reaches the Breast Hill summit, but press on to reach that summit and the views are superb. The Cardrona Fault has sliced the land in front at a steep angle, and from this hanging vantage, you look down on Lake Hawea, the toy township at the foot of the lake, and out over the Hawea and Wanaka basins. For Te Araroa walkers headed south, this is the memorable entry onto Otago.

Beyond the summit, the track is mostly unformed and hugs a fence line as it descends to the new eight-bunk Pakituhi Hut (1300 m). The hut was put in to serve Te Araroa trampers and whatever day or overnight walkers might come up from Lake Hawea. (Distance 11 km.)

4. Pakituhi Hut to Gladstone Reserve. The track makes a steep, 950 m descent to Timaru Creek Rd, initially along the ridgeline to a small saddle, then scrambling down a steep face on a zigzagging route. It's a challenging last leg. (Distance 5 km.)

Turn left at the road, and the Gladstone Reserve is lakeside about 1 km distant.

ew over Lake Hawea from Breast Hill, Breast Hill Track.

kituhi Hut, Breast Hill Track.

THE TRACK STARTS AT GLADSTONE, a small settlement of mainly holiday homes at the Johns Creek outlet onto Lake Hawea. From Gladstone Reserve follow a scenic clifftop and lakefront route through, until you strike the Lake Hawea Hotel. It has a bar and restaurant, and it's close to the town centre.

Lake Hawea village is the least commercial of the three lakeside towns on Te Araroa's route. It's a beautiful spot, and there's only around 1000 people resident in the area. The town has a reputation as a cycle- and walker-friendly place, opposed in its public meetings to any large-scale development, or such imports from the outside world as chain stores or chain restaurants.

GLADSTONE TRACK

NORTHERN START	Gladstone Reserve
SOUTHERN END	Lake Hawea township
DISTANCE	6.5 km
MAPS	120
TRACK STANDARD	Easy tramping

THE HAWEA RIVER TRACK was the first track put in place by the Upper Clutha Tracks Trust and was opened and signed into Te Araroa's route in 2009. From the Hawea River control gates, follow Domain Rd 800 m to a junction with Cemetery Rd, and a side track down to the river, which drains Lake Hawea with a wide, steady flow before debouching into the Clutha. The track follows along beside it for 11 km on a wide, hard-packed aggregate surface then crosses it on a 70 metre swing bridge. The bridge is wider than the usual tramping bridges to accommodate bikes and prams, though they have to be carried down the steps at the southern end. The path then follows vehicle tracks to the Hawea–Albert Town Rd, and crosses the road to finish at the Albert Town Reserve campground.

Cross the Clutha River on the road bridge, and turn right onto the Outlet Track.

HAWEA RIVER TRACK

NORTHERN START	Domain Rd, Lake Hawea township
SOUTHERN END	Albert Town Reserve
DISTANCE	12 km
MAPS	120
TRACK STANDARD	Easy tramping

OUTLET TRACK

NORTHERN START	Clutha River bridge
SOUTHERN END	Wanaka
DISTANCE	12 km
MAPS	120, 121
TRACK STANDARD	Easy tramping

THE TRACK BEGINS AT THE SOUTH END (the Albert Town end) of the Clutha River bridge. Turn right and follow the Clutha upriver on a tree-lined path 6 km to its source — the outflow at Lake Wanaka. Even here the Clutha looks a god among rivers. It's strong enough to roll boulders, and already hints at the arterial strength that will make it, by tonnage, New Zealand's greatest river.

Beyond Beacon Point, the route then stitches in local tracks along the lake shoreline to finish at Wanaka's lakeside shops and cafés. Wanaka has every type of accommodation and its outdoors shops confirm its place at the heart of tramping, climbing and skiing country. It's often compared with the larger Queenstown for adventure potential, but is somewhat more austere and serious about it. It's the closest town to the entry to Mt Aspiring National Park, and the climbers who tackle Mt Aspiring come through this gateway. The town has pleasingly eccentric touches like the car seats and couches in its cinema, and perhaps the only Masonic hall in the world where the Masonic symbol of square and compass is set with the spikes of the compass pointing upwards.

GLENDHU BAY TRACK

NORTHERN START	Wanaka
SOUTHERN END	Glendhu Bay
DISTANCE	15 km
MAPS	121, 122
TRACK STANDARD	Easy tramping

THE TRAIL HEADS WEST around the lakeshore, passing under tall poplars as it departs the township into the grassy lakeside reserves beyond. Glaciers close to 1 km high once pushed out of the Matukituki Valley west of the lake, and the Makaroa Valley at its head. The township is built on glacial till, and as you look back, Mt Iron, the staunch rock at the back of town, is a classic *roche moutonnée*, one flank eroded obliquely by glacial advance, but dropping away steeply on the lee. Past Waterfall Creek, the lake opens up onto hummocky islands and peninsulas, terrain also smoothed and eroded long ago by the glacial advance.

It's all melted back now into a placid and reflective lake spread out below Roys Peak. The track offers viewpoints from bluffs above the lake as well as shoreline encounters with it, ending with a final lakeside walk into Glendhu Bay and the campground there.

The Wanaka–Mount Aspiring Rd runs along the back of the Glendhu Bay campground. Turn left from this road into Motatapu Rd and follow the gravel road margin to the Fern Burn car park, which marks the start of the Motatapu Alpine Track.

uth end of Lake Hawea, Gladstone Track.

spension Bridge, Hawea River, Hawea River Track.

MUTT AND EILEEN LANGE agreed this Te Araroa route in 2004 as part of their purchase agreement for the Motatapu and Mt Soho Station pastoral leases, together totalling 225 sq km.

For many years Te Araroa Trust had sought a route to connect Wanaka and Macetown, and followed up rumours of a purchase offer on Motatapu Station with a request to the Overseas Investment Office that a route be part of any sale. The two music millionaires, he a producer, she a Canadian country singer whose stage name is Shania Twain, confirmed they'd not just accept a track easement, they'd fund construction and two 12-person huts en route. Later they added a third hut.

Prime Minister Helen Clark opened the track in 2008, and it quickly gained a reputation as a hard tramp. DOC added 'alpine' into the title to flag the fact the track is usually unformed, crosses exposed terrain and has steep climbs and ankle-testing sidles. It's hot in summer but winter conditions can blow in any time of year, and winter brings snow. Trampers need back-country experience, warm windproof clothing and stout footwear. They should carry water and sunblock.

1. Fern Burn car park to Fern Burn Hut. The track leads off through deer paddocks on the Fern Burn's true right, then ascends through beech forest beside the rock pools of the tumbling Fern Burn before breaking into tussock and following a nicely benched track to the hut. It's a one-day return walk if you want to taste the territory. (Distance 7 km.)

2. Fern Burn Hut to Highland Creek Hut. Follow marker poles up the Fern Burn to Jack Hall's Saddle (1275 m) before a swift descent on a ridge that drops 400 m in altitude in just over 1 km. The track crosses a creek, then two more spurs to enter beneath the bluffs of the Highland Creek catchment to the 12-person Highland Creek Hut. (Distance 6 km.)

3. Highland Creek Hut to Roses Hut. The demanding section of the track has two climbs where you gain, then lose, around 450 m of height. DOC suggests it's a six- to eight-hour section.

Soon after leaving the hut, the first climb starts with a zigzag up a crumbling spur that hardens up but remains steep through to Knuckle Peak's northwest ridge.

MOTATAPU ALPINE TRACK

NORTHERN START	Fern Burn car park
SOUTHERN END	Macetown
DISTANCE	34 km
MAPS	122, 123
TRACK STANDARD	Hard tramping

An easy sidle downwards from there turns into a sharp descent where you'll find the grandfather tussock useful as handholds. The track bottoms out onto a tree-shaded creek then climbs again, this time up Knuckle Peak's southwestern ridge. Above stands the bony western face of Knuckle Peak. This is high country at its most raw: silence upon the rock and the tussock holding the swarming patterns of the wind.

Once you've gained the southwest ridge, travel is all downhill along a fence line that sings if the wind is blowing, and is a handhold if the wind is blowing really hard. Once in the valley, cross the gravelly bed of the Motatapu River to the 12-person Roses Hut. (Distance 11 km.)

4. Roses Hut to Macetown. Follow the old packhorse track to Roses Saddle (1270 m). From the saddle the pack track fades to a shadow, but there are orange-topped markers, and glimpses through to the Remarkables Range beyond Queenstown. It's a long descent but you can shortcut finally to the Arrow River if it's at normal to low flow and follow it down to Macetown. Otherwise, the poled high-water track sidles down to cross the river opposite the old gold-mining ghost town — population zero. (Distance 10 km.)

BIG HILL TRACK

NORTHERN START	Macetown
SOUTHERN END	Arrowtown
DISTANCE	12 km
MAPS	123, 124
TRACK STANDARD	Tramping

BEFORE THE ROAD WAS BUILT in the 1880s, the Big Hill Track was the packhorse route to Macetown. Follow the 4WD road 1.5 km downstream to the Eight Mile/Coronet Creek confluence, head up the creek for 500 m then follow poles leading off on the true right up to Big Hill Saddle (1060 m) and good views across the Wakatipu Basin. The formed track descends through open tussock country and beech forest down to the Sawpit Gully Trail junction, where it takes the right-hand track and exits to Arrowtown on the Bush Creek Trail to Ramshaw Lane.

Big Hill Track is exposed and in poor weather, river levels permitting, trampers can stay on the 4WD road out to Arrowtown.

ampers climbing to Jack Hall's Saddle, Motatapu Alpine Track.

THIS TRACK SPANS the Wakatipu Basin between Arrowtown and Lake Wakatipu on footpaths, cycle tracks and even through a golf resort. It may attract those who like unusual exploration. The track passes through the Millbrook Resort, links to the restored Lower Shotover Bridge, and undertakes a final, interesting journey past Queenstown's relegations — the dog pound, the oxidation ponds, the transfer station.

NORTHERN START	Arrowtown
SOUTHERN END	Frankton Domain
DISTANCE	22 km
MAPS	124, 125
TRACK STANDARD	Easy tramping

The track starts in Arrowtown near Ramshaw Lane/ Buckingham St/Berkshire St intersection. Walk up Berkshire, turn right into Wiltshire St then right again into Caernarvon St. This street continues into Manse Rd. Follow the roadside track here past Butal Park to the Malaghans Rd intersection. Turn right onto Malaghans Rd and left onto Millbrook Track a short distance later, just before The Avenue, the main road entry into the Millbrook Resort.

The Millbrook Track is just over 3 km long and marked. It runs alongside The Avenue to the resort centre then veers to the right to follow Mill Stream and pass through Coronet Nine golf course. The track then exits onto Speargrass Flat Rd. Turn right here and then left into Slope Hill Rd, and left again into Rutherford Rd and down to the carpark at Lake Hayes.

From the carpark the route veers right onto the track down the western side of the lake, before crossing SH6 into Lake Hayes Estate.

Te Araroa joins the Queenstown Cycle Trail, following the Kawarau River's true left, then heads up the Shotover River to the historic Lower Shotover Bridge — completed in 1915 after a shoddy start, when a bridge contractor failed to build the specified footings, and a Shotover flood took out a bridge pier. The bridge fell into neglect last century, but was renovated in 2005 by the Rotary Shotover Bridge Restoration Trust, which replaced the deck and handrails.

Cross the bridge and go left onto a track that heads down towards the river and passes under the highway bridge. Take the first right past the dog pound and the gun club towards the locked gate to the oxidation ponds. Follow the track on the right-hand side up the terrace onto Glenda Drive.

Cross the drive, turn left and then quickly right down a narrow path between commercial properties. That comes out opposite a hardware 'big-box' store. Go right here, then left and down to the roundabout. Go right again, then just before the next roundabout take a left onto the shared cycle- and walkway running parallel to the main road. Follow this past new retail developments around the edge of Queenstown Events Centre to Joe O'Connell Drive. Continue past the pool entrance and car park onto a tarsealed path that leads away from the Events Centre to your right through the golf course. Cross State Highway 6, turn right, then left into Ross St, right down McBride St, left down Birse St and through to the Frankton Domain.

FRANKTON ARM WALKWAY

NORTHERN START	Frankton Domain
SOUTHERN END	Queenstown
DISTANCE	8 km
MAPS	124, 125
TRACK STANDARD	Easy tramping

FROM THE FRANKTON DOMAIN a wide and social track leads away along the lakefront with good views out to the Remarkables, Cecil Peak and Kelvin Peninsula, then ends on Park St. Continue along Park St to pick up the tracks around Queenstown Gardens to the Queenstown lakefront.

The town is beautiful, it's famous, it's tucked into very steep terrain. Gondolas loop uphill, parapenters hang overhead, ski roads slant upward on grim rock to snowcapped peaks, and down on the lake, the vintage steamer *Earnslaw* sends up a plume of coal smoke. Perfect.

Lake Wakatipu now forms a natural break. The next trailhead is the Greenstone Wharf, 41 km by boat up Lake Wakatipu. As with Cook Strait, this is a wide water break, though if the trail is gauged by continuous latitude, there is no interruption. Queenstown is at 45° 02' 00" and the Greenstone Wharf is at 44° 56' 20" — an eighth of a degree north. Charter boats operate directly from Queenstown to the Greenstone Wharf, but are expensive. A cheap alternative is to take a road shuttle to Glenorchy, then a water taxi to the Greenstone Wharf, or attempt to hitch via Kinloch.

ake Wakatipu and the Remarkables from Frankton Arm Walkway.

southland

THE LAND

The wrinkled expanse of Fiordland gets famously drenched by rain coming from the west, and its huge lakes are usually brimming. Even the seawater in the fiords is overlain often with fresh water, but if there's a rain shadow affecting Southland, you'd hardly notice. Much of Southland's weather arrives out of the unprotected southwest corner, straight off the ocean. The region can get wet, and its southern coast can get windy. Foveaux Strait amplifies the westerlies almost as much as that other great wind funnel, Cook Strait.

Te Araroa enters Southland through the long Mararoa Valley, slips through a gap in the Takitimu Mountains and gains the Longwood Range. As with Fiordland, the Longwoods are hard rock, not uprisen under pressure like the Takitimus but a plutonic slug out of Gondwana, old and worn down, with placer gold at their foot.

The Southland Downs inland and the Southland Plains that run to the coast form a green and highly productive lowland, and Te Araroa goes around the edges of it, along Oreti Beach and down the long New River Estuary to pick its way finally across the granite boulders of Bluff Hill.

THE PEOPLE

Maori knew the region as Murihiku, and gave it a memorable mythology. The Takitimu Range is a migration waka wrecked in Te Waewae Bay, the Hokonui Range 60 km east its bailing

Southland Downs, near Tapanui.

figure, the large, round, rocky protuberance 60 km south on the Orepuke coast its anchor stone. Whalers and sealers settled here and cleaned it out. The last rising of that extractive-industry flame was the Invercargill factory that refined elephant seal and penguin oil.

The Scots were the dominant immigrants and they raised a pastoral and dairy economy, planned a city with wide, flat streets, brought in piped water, gas street lighting and trams, and built the First Presbyterian Church with a million bricks. It's as if someone forgot to tell Southland that civilisation rarely thrives in such latitudes.

Scottish order is evident right through the region, in the trim box hedges, and the roads edged with flax that are comparatively clear of the usual splatter from stock trucks, even on Gypsy Day. Southland's dairy farmers are reckoned the country's best at standing their stock.

The past is stoically preserved in a display of 56 clan tartans, but Southland's deep south latitudes, its unobstructed horizons and low radio noise make it an advanced outpost for tracking European rocket launches, receiving data downloads from polar satellites, and for future galactic science.

Te Araroa's route goes through Invercargill at the outlying Stead Street Wharf, but there are great cafés in the city centre, and restaurants that serve, in season from March to June, Bluff oysters. When walkers explore further in they may perhaps spot one secret of Invercargill's staunch success. Beneath the stainless-steel umbrella sculpture aslant in Dee St are hundreds of ceremonial bricks that note by name the families who live in Invercargill. Not many cities could do that, or possibly even think of it.

LIVINGSTONE MOUNTAINS

to Mavora Lakes road end

North Mavora Lake

Careys Hut

Windon Burn

Boundary Hut

Mt Mavora 1990

Von River (north)

Mararoa River

THOMSON MOUNTAINS

Mavora Lakes
Walkway

Mararoa River

Taipo Hut

Pond Burn

Pass Burn
Saddle

Pass Burn

Greenstone River

Sly Burn

Tooth Peak 2061

AILSA MOUNTAINS

Greenstone Hut

bridge

Slip Flat Hut

Slip Flat

Lake Wakatipu

201°

bridge

Greenstone River

Caples River

Pig Island / Matau

Greenstone Wharf

Greenstone Station Rd

Pigeon Island / Wawahi Waka

N

GREENSTONE STATION RD leads away from the Greenstone Wharf, 2 km to the car park. Greenstone Station, on your left, is owned by Ngai Tahu, the largest of the South Island tribes, and the track ahead is one of the old routes used by Maori from the deep south to and from Te Wai Pounamu's western coast and its greenstone lodes. In the late 1990s, as part of the settlement of nineteenth-century land grievances with the Crown, Ngai Tahu reasserted its mana whenua status here, with purchases of the sheep and cattle stations around the top of Lake Wakatipu and along these valleys.

The New Zealand Walkways Commission in the 1970s had as one of its goals a trail from end to end of New Zealand. It was the first New Zealand organisation with a warrant to put in tracks, called 'Walkways' under the NZWC legislation. The commission didn't achieve the end-to-end goal, but it made a start, and the track ahead is one of its north–south routes. You'll see the old Walkways symbol on some of the posts en route — an orange 'W' with a symbolic white path winding towards the W's central apex.

The Mavora Lakes Walkway, despite that soothing suggestion in the track name of a walk in the park, is a traditional tramp with hazards. Streams that tumble off mountain ranges along the way can be steep and fast after rain, and back-country skills are useful here.

1. Greenstone Station Rd road-end to Greenstone Hut.
From the car park the track climbs above the Greenstone River then descends to a swing bridge near the Caples River confluence. It follows the Greenstone River on a well-formed path through beech forest, then narrows to a gorge beneath the steep-sided flanks of the Ailsa Mountains. There's a winter avalanche danger around the first of the steep stream catchments here, and at Slip Flat there's an emergency bridge across a creek flowing out of another of those steep catchments, prone to flood. The next swing bridge has clear signage to turn you left across the Greenstone River, to a grassy clearing beneath the rock pinnacles of Tooth Peak and the 20-bunk Greenstone Hut. (Distance 11 km.)

MAVORA LAKES WALKWAY (STAGE 1)

NORTHERN START	Greenstone Wharf
SOUTHERN END	Boundary Hut
DISTANCE	34 km
MAPS	128, 129
TRACK STANDARD	Tramping

2. Greenstone Hut to Taipo Hut. The Mavora Lakes Track leaves the Greenstone River in Otago territory and sidles into Southland across a soft beech-forest floor, emerging onto a bog pine glade with striking views back up the Greenstone Valley. The first stream crossing is a boulder-hop of the gushing Pass Burn. Waratahs then mark out a steep climb to the Pass Burn Saddle (728 m).

Beyond the saddle the track stays in forest for a time then drops down over a terrace into the tussock lands just opposite the middle of the top pond. From here, tall tussock can make track markers hard to see. Be aware also if you're navigating with old LINZ 260 series 1:50,000 maps that Taipo Hut is wrongly positioned by almost a kilometre. The replacement LINZ NZTopo50 series has corrected the site.

Stay on the true right of the Pond Burn and stick close to the toe of the range to get to the hut. It's tucked in below a terrace beside the Mararoa River, fenced and with admission through a turntable made from an old cartwheel. The track is crossing Elfin Bay Station, another Ngai Tahu property, so there are cattle to be kept at bay. (Distance 10 km.)

3. Taipo Hut to Boundary Hut. Cross the Mararoa River on a swing bridge, and the track goes on across river terraces, crossing a series of side streams off the long flanks of the highest peak en route, Mt Mavora (1990 m). It weaves on over the terraces and between flatland bogs to cross another swing bridge over the Mararoa to the four-bunk Boundary Hut. The tramp across Elfin Bay Station land ends, and from here to the Mavora Lakes, inclusive of the hut, DOC has opened up a general recreation area to four-wheel-drives, motorcycle riders, horse riders, and mountain bikers. (Distance 13 km.)

Through-tramper fording Pass Burn, Mavora Lakes Walkway.

North Mavora Lake, Mavora Lakes Walkway.

4. Boundary Hut to Mavora Lakes campground. From Boundary Hut, follow the four-wheel-drive track for 6 km down to Careys Hut on the North Mavora Lake shoreline, then along the lake edge another 7 km. Beech forest offers a shaded final 3 km alongside the lake, before you emerge onto the campground. There's no regular public transport out of this area, but in summer there'll be day-trippers and anglers making the most of this beauty spot and its trout fishing. (Distance 16 km.)

Walk down to the swing bridge at the North Mavora Lake outlet.

MAVORA LAKES WALKWAY (STAGE 2)

NORTHERN START	Boundary Hut
SOUTHERN END	Mavora Lakes campground
DISTANCE	16 km
MAPS	129, 130
TRACK STANDARD	Tramping

CROSS THE SWING BRIDGE at the North Mavora Lake outlet, and follow the South Mavora Lake shoreline south to rejoin the Mararoa River. Stay on the true right 7 km to the Kiwi Burn access bridge. Here there's a choice of staying on the true right of the river or crossing the bridge to the true left.

The 12-bunk Kiwi Burn Hut is 5 km distant at this point, on the Mararoa's true right. It can be part of the trail but only if you're confident of your ability to ford the Mararoa opposite the hut and pick up the true left track again that way. TAT will try to secure a swing bridge nearer to the Kiwi Burn Hut to make this an all-weather route, but meantime this is our best suggestion; if you want to use the Kiwi Burn Hut, your arrival at the Kiwi Burn bridge gives you the chance to assess the Mararoa's flow, and decide whether the river has a low enough summer flow to be fordable if you come into it, unbridged, from the hut.

Having crossed the access bridge (or having forded the river further down) continue down the river's true left to Wash Creek, ford the creek and, to avoid being bluffed, return to Mavora Lakes Rd. Follow along 3.5 km to an anglers' access and return to the river through to Mararoa Rd. Bulls often graze this paddock so take care and leave the gate as found.

From Mararoa Rd south, you're on Burwood Station. The station has granted access to trampers during daylight hours, but there's no camping, no dogs, no fires, and no firearms allowed. Follow through to the anglers' access leading up to State Highway 94 and Princhester Rd.

MARAROA RIVER TRACK

NORTHERN START	North Mavora Lake outlet
SOUTHERN END	SH 94 at Princhester Rd
DISTANCE	47 km
MAPS	130, 131, 132
TRACK STANDARD	Tramping

WHETHER DRESSED IN WINTER WHITE or summer brown, the Takitimu Range is one of Southland's most revered landscapes. Ngai Tahu has placed a spiritual cloak over the range, and the Southland Tramping Club knows it as a benign alpine environment, with handy huts and bivvies built by the New Zealand Forest Service in the 1960s. Te Araroa enters the range over a saddle to the Upper Aparima Valley, journeys along the base of the massif, climbs high into the foothills and descends to the Waitaki Valley.

In the past, the range has had only two legal entrance points, Princhester Rd and Dunrobin Rd. TAT has negotiated a third, through Mt Linton Station, for the last 19 km of its through-tramp, but it's not access as of right, and trampers going through this last section of the track must abide by special conditions:

- Tramping parties must never be larger than eight people.
- Use the track only in daylight hours.
- Always stick to the track and use stiles as provided.
- Give way to farm/forestry operations.
- No camping, fires, vehicles including bikes, horses, dogs, or firearms.
- Carry out all rubbish.
- No commercial activity, including guiding or organised events.

Three huts exist en route, but it's usually a four-day track and trampers should carry the necessary tent or bivvy bag for one night camping out beyond the Lower Wairaki Hut. The route is new, and though it's marked throughout there's often no visible ground trail. This will improve as the track gets greater use, but meantime trampers should have back-country experience and carry maps and a compass. A GPS is very handy for this track. The track line is on GPX files that can be downloaded from TAT's website.

1. State Highway 94 to Lower Princhester Hut. From the highway the route follows the gravelled Princhester Rd, a public road but also a working farm access. Dogs are not permitted, and you should give way to stock and farm operations and leave gates as you find them. The road dwindles to a rough farm track and reaches DOC's six-bunk Lower Princhester Hut just beyond the treeline. (Distance 6 km.)

TAKITIMU TRACK (STAGE 1)

NORTHERN START	Princhester Rd
SOUTHERN END	Lower Wairaki Hut
DISTANCE	63 km total. This stage 36 km.
MAPS	132, 133
TRACK STANDARD	Hard tramping Closed for lambing, 25 September– 5 November inclusive

2. Lower Princhester Hut to Aparima Hut. The track climbs through beech forest on the true right of the Bog Burn to a 780 m saddle between the Takitimu's northernmost peak, Mt Hamilton (1487 m), and Mt Clare (1490 m) on the main range. It then descends to the Waterloo Burn and the northern boundary of Waterloo Station, a Crown Pastoral Lease comprising 3500 hectares. It's about 4.5 km to this point.

Waterloo Station allows tramper access down its western boundary. The route is poled through tussock land on the fringe of the forest, and marked across the forested headlands. The GPX file is often useful to keep you on the permitted track line during this long route through to the 12-bunk Aparima Hut. Even if you arrive at the hut with sufficient daylight hours to go on, you're wise to consider an overnight stop here to start refreshed in the morning. The next section calls for careful progress. (Distance 17 km.)

3. Aparima Hut to Lower Wairaki Hut. Descend to the swing bridge and cross the Aparima River. The track then forks to Dunrobin Rd left, and Te Araroa right. Dunrobin Rd is a bypass if the Mt Linton section ahead is closed for lambing.

Te Araroa's route is poled onward, west through spongy marshland above the Aparima River's true right bank to the forest. Here the route slows right up and will remain so until a recognisable ground trail is tramped into place.

The unformed track rolls over the foothills in this manner to a signposted junction with the Wairaki River track, an established track that's easier to follow. Turn left and follow it downstream to a marked ford. Cross the river here as river levels allow and climb to the four-bunk Lower Wairaki Hut. (Distance 13 km.)

akitimu Mountains, from Mararoa River Track.

elford Burn, Takitimu Track.

4. Lower Wairaki Hut to Telford Burn. The track departs the hut to traverse the bush fringe to a stream — the last potable water en route. A marker here points the way up a steepening slope to the ridgeline. Follow along the ridge for 440 m to emerge on the tops, with excellent views towards the south coast. Marker poles lead away down the main ridge for 2 km before the track leaves the ridge to the right and descends through grasslands to the Telford Burn campsite, which has a toilet and stream water. (Distance 8 km.)

5. Telford Burn to Struan Flat Rd. Note: this section crosses the privately owned Mt Linton Station. Please comply with all conditions set down for access through this property. The generosity of the landowners deserves reciprocal respect, and Te Araroa will lose this critical link if the conditions are broken, including these requests:

- To comply with the condition for daylight passage only, trampers should leave Telford Burn no later than midday and make steady progress towards the exit to Mt Linton.
- Farm vehicles and stock movement have absolute right of way. Step aside and wait quietly until all livestock has passed.
- Please take direction from farm staff as necessary.

There's no potable water available en route so trampers should carry sufficient water to last the day. From the campsite, follow the poled route down the true left side of Telford Burn to a signposted crossing. Ford the river here, as river levels allow, onto a farm track to cross the Wairaki River on a swing bridge. The marked track beyond joins a farm road near Rock Hut — a private hut unavailable to trampers.

Follow the road for 12 km to a junction marked by the Douglas Charles Nunn memorial. Turn left here and 400 m down the road cross left on a stile and follow poles along fence lines to a bridge across Morley Stream and the Struan Flat Rd trailhead just beyond. Cell phones work from Struan Flat Rd and trampers can phone to nearby Ohai if they need shuttle transport or accommodation. Details are on TAT's website. (Distance 19 km.)

TAKITIMU TRACK (STAGE 2)

NORTHERN START	Lower Wairaki Hut
SOUTHERN END	Struan Flat Rd
DISTANCE	63 km total. This stage 27 km.
MAPS	133, 134
TRACK STANDARD	Hard tramping Closed for lambing 25 September– 5 November inclusive

- Tramping parties must never be larger than eight people.
- Use the track only in daylight hours.
- Always stick to the track and use stiles as provided.
- Give way to farm/forestry operations.
- No camping, fires, vehicles including bikes, horses, dogs, or firearms.
- Carry out all rubbish.
- No commercial activity, including guiding or organised events.

WOODLAW TRACK

NORTHERN START	Struan Flat Rd
SOUTHERN END	Scotts Gap–Feldwick Rd
DISTANCE	19 km
MAPS	134, 135
TRACK STANDARD	Tramping
	Closed for lambing 9 September to 9 November inclusive

- Tramping parties must never be larger than eight people.
- Use the track only in daylight hours.
- Always stick to the track and use stiles as provided.
- Give way to farm/forestry operations.
- No camping, fires, vehicles including bikes, horses, dogs, or firearms.
- Carry out all rubbish.
- No commercial activity, including guiding or organised events.

THIS TRACK IS ALMOST ENTIRELY on private property and ongoing access is dependent upon the goodwill of three landowners: Birchwood Station, Matariki Forests, and D.T. King & Co Ltd. Please comply with all conditions set down for access through these properties. The generosity of the landowners deserves reciprocal respect, and Te Araroa will lose this critical link if the conditions are broken, including these requests:

- To comply with the condition for daylight passage only, trampers should start out early in the morning, and make steady progress towards the Woodlaw Track exit.
- Moving stock have absolute right of way. Step aside and wait quietly until all livestock has passed.
- Please take direction from farm staff as necessary.

Follow markers from Struan Flat Rd to Birchwood–Wairio Rd, coming to a eucalypt plantation where the route skirts around the western then southern edge of this. Beyond the plantation, cross the stock lane on a left-hand diagonal. The track then climbs gently beside a stream to the base of the Twinlaw Range, follows right on a steep, grassy farm track up to the main ridge, then travels left along the ridgeline to the Birchwood Station/Twinlaw Forest boundary gate.

Beyond the gate a four-wheel-drive track leads away through exotic forest. Te Araroa markers guide you onto Trig Rd then Twinlaw Rd. Leave Twinlaw Rd finally on a four-wheel-drive exit that leads away right to the Twinlaw/Woodlaw Forest Boundary and a turning bay there. The track then heads away through beech forest towards Woodlaw Peak, then descends for 2 km to a narrow strip of exotic forest. It joins the main four-wheel-drive track through to its junction with a forest road which leads out of the forest onto a long, fenced straight through farmland to the Scotts Gap–Feldwick Road.

Turn left down the road, and the next right-hand bend leads onto a long straight. Hewitt Road is 2 km down on the right.

THIS TRACK IS ENTIRELY on private property and the two landowners, Matariki Forests and Mike Whale, have granted access. Please comply with all conditions set down for passage through these properties. The generosity of the landowners deserves reciprocal respect, and Te Araroa will lose this critical link if the conditions are broken, including these requests:

- To comply with the condition for daylight passage only, trampers should start out early in the morning and make steady progress towards the Island Block Track exit.
- Moving stock have absolute right of way. Step aside and wait quietly until all livestock has passed.
- Please take direction from farm staff as necessary.

The track starts at the forest-entry gate near the top of Hewitt Rd. If arriving by car, park near the bottom of Hewitt Rd and walk up. Beyond the gate, Hewitt Rd continues into the forest to a junction with Loop Rd. Turn left, then turn left again at the next junction. At each of the last two junctions, take the right fork.

From the road-end, the track leads between pine tree rows to the farmland boundary. This is the section that requires prior permission from the farm manager to cross. Once across the boundary fence, turn left downhill on the farm track. Markers guide you across a paddock and along a shelterbelt. Go through the gate and continue on a farm track leading through a second shelterbelt to a roadside gate.

Walk right along the Otautau–Tuatapere Road 1.5 km, then turn left into Merrivale Rd and walk up to the Longwood Forest Track.

ISLAND BUSH TRACK

NORTHERN START	Hewitt Rd
SOUTHERN END	Otautau–Tuatapere Rd
DISTANCE	4 km
MAPS	135
TRACK STANDARD	Tramping

- Tramping parties must never be larger than eight people.
- Use the track only in daylight hours.
- Always stick to the track and use stiles as provided.
- Give way to farm/forestry operations.
- No camping, fires, vehicles including bikes, horses, dogs, or firearms.
- Carry out all rubbish.
- No commercial activity, including guiding or organised events.

THE LONGWOOD RANGE clouds in frequently, and when it does the poled route on the tops can be hard to find. The only hut en route is both primitive and 28 km distant, so trampers unable to complete the long first leg should calculate where they'd camp. Back-country experience, warm windproof clothing, maps, a compass and a GPS are advisable. It's a serious tramp. (See map on page 262 for track start.)

Merrivale Rd turns into a forest road after 4 km, and becomes progressively more impassable to wheeled traffic, including four-wheel-drives. Stay on the gravelled track — at the first junction Merrivale Rd continues left, at the second it continues right. About 3.5 km into the forest the road ends and a four-wheel-drive track takes you through to the tramping track.

The ground trail isn't obvious but orange track markers lead on through beech forest up a fairly gentle ridge that steepens abruptly before a poled entry onto the rounded summit of Bald Hill (805 m) and its transmission tower.

Follow the access road down for 3 km to an abandoned quarry. An old New Zealand Forest Service sign of riddled metal marks the track entrance to Little Baldy (745 m).

From Little Baldy onward, the Longwood tops provide a great poled walk through subalpine shrubbery, and a bare, tussocked ridge to the Longwood trig (764 m). The view is panoramic — east over the green plains of Southland, south to Stewart Island's Mt Anglem, and west to Te Waewae Bay and Fiordland's Princess Mountains.

The poled route goes on to Pt 748 before bending east, down to the treeline and a descent through thick forest to the three-bed Martins Hut. The hut dates back to 1905 and housed one of the Longwoods' water-race maintenance men. It's had some preservation work, but remains a fairly unreconstructed delight with a dirt floor, and hessian sacking lining the bunks.

The track continues downhill to a forest road. Turn right onto the road, then left onto Cascade Rd and continue downhill for just over 1 km to the start of the Ports water race leg.

In the 1890s the Chinese set up their own town at Round Hill, 22 km distant from here, and washed gold out of the gravel banks. European companies moved in later with plans for larger-scale hydraulic mining. Charles Port contracted the Chinese to dig this water race supplying the dams poised above Round Hill — a pressure head for the sluicing nozzles below.

LONGWOOD FOREST TRACK

NORTHERN START	Merrivale Rd
SOUTHERN END	Round Hill Rd
DISTANCE	54 km
MAPS	135, 136, 137
TRACK STANDARD	Hard tramping

You're now walking the maintenance track beside a race that tunnelled through spurs and was once supported across gullies on trestles, falling only a minimal few metres every kilometre to keep the water gently flowing. The water-race corridor was exempt from milling, so mature rimu, kamahi, and totara trees overhang the track.

LONG HILLY TRACK

NORTHERN START	Ports water race
SOUTHERN END	Round Hill Rd
DISTANCE	1.5 km (3 km loop track)
MAPS	137
TRACK STANDARD	Easy tramping

THE LONG HILLY TRACK is an integral part of the Longwood Forest Track but is broken out here as a good stand-alone loop track that can be accessed from its southern end by day-walkers at the Round Hill Rd car park. Through-trampers access it from the northern end, turning left at the old dams, and passing through a tramway cutting, past old alluvial test holes, a remnant sluicing pipe, and Chinese stonework before reaching the car park.

Walk down Round Hill Rd to the Riverton Highway to Colac Bay, which has a campground, a backpackers' lodge, and the Colac Bay Tavern.

TIHAKA BEACH TRACK

NORTHERN START	Colac Bay
SOUTHERN END	Riverton
DISTANCE	10 km
MAPS	137, 138
TRACK STANDARD	Tramping

WALK THE COLAC BAY FORESHORE and go on past the first rocky headland. This end of the bay is known as Tihaka Beach. From here the marked track passes up and over several headlands before returning to the beach. Continue on the marked route through a deer fence, then follow the markers up the ridge towards Mores Reserve. From the bush edge, follow an access track for about 250 m. A stile here takes you over the fence to join the track system in the reserve through to the car park. The reserve has had a 'pest-busters' programme going for years, begun by local stalwart Warrick McCallum, and as you look out over Riverton you may hear a tui singing.

Look over your shoulder occasionally, back towards the Longwood Range. Local advice is that if the Longwoods look to be turning blue, rain is not far away — you've been warned!

Go down Richard St to Riverton and through to Oreti Beach.

Through-tramper Johno Tunnell with gold mining relics, Longwood Forest Track.

Colac Bay, Tihaka Beach Track.

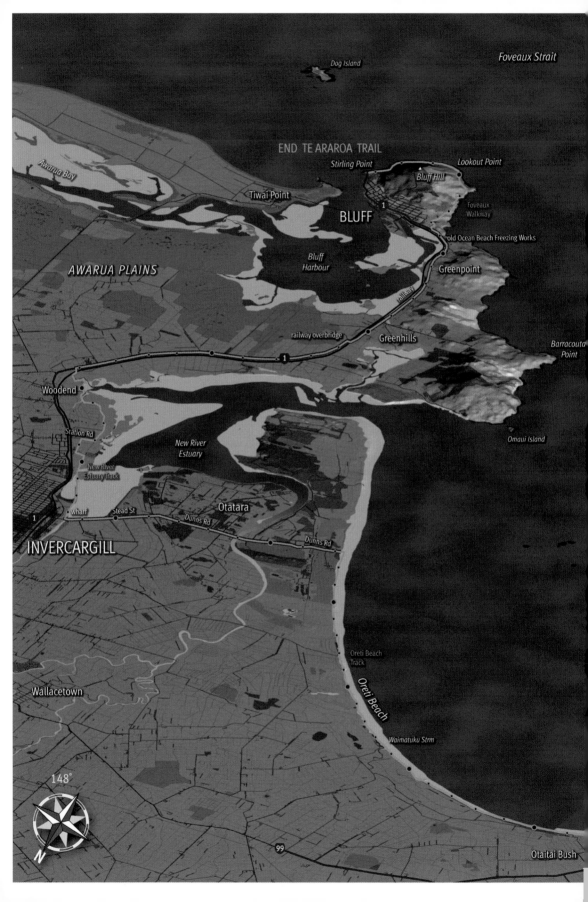

FROM THE NORTH SIDE of the estuary bridge, turn down Jetty St and keep going. A riverside track beside a line of pine trees leads to the beach. (See map on page 266 for track start.)

It's then a 21 km walk along the curving swathe of Oreti Beach. Twelve kilometres on, the Waimatuku Stream flows across the beach, and can be difficult to cross, but only when the tide is high and the stream backs up.

Stewart Island Rakiura is a blue silhouette on the southern horizon, the green marram grass of the dunes is on your left, and there's high land out to the southeast but Bluff is not yet in sight. This penultimate walk, if you read the web journals of Te Araroa through-walkers, is a time for contemplation of last things. It's Te Araroa's last beach walk, and the last tramping day but one. Distant figures start to appear, and maybe cars — the beach is a popular destination for Invercargillites.

Dunns Rd, Te Araroa's turnoff toward Invercargill, is obvious when you get to it. The road is marked by a power pole with a streetlight and a Te Araroa finger sign that points inland, to the last 9 km footpaths that join with Stead St and cross the New River Estuary to the Stead St Wharf.

ORETI BEACH TRACK

NORTHERN START	Riverton
SOUTHERN END	Stead St Wharf
DISTANCE	30 km
MAPS	138, 139, 140
TRACK STANDARD	Easy tramping

THIS DUAL-PURPOSE CYCLEWAY and walking track is being steadily extended, with Te Araroa Trust providing a significant contribution to the first completed stage. At present it runs from the Stead St Wharf on a flat aggregate path and along the edge of the New River Estuary. Keep an eye out for seasonal bird life as the trail runs to Kekeno Place and rejoins State Highway 1 just before the Ballance Agri-Nutrients factory. Then, there's no immediate alternative to a 15 km road-walk south along State Highway 1.

Exit from Kekeno Place onto State Highway 1 and walk to Ocean Beach. Seven kilometres beyond Awarua, State Highway 1 rises and curves away right on an overbridge across the railway line. Don't walk this bridge, it's dangerous. Three hundred metres before the bridge, there's an informal lay-by on the right-hand side. This connects to a portion of the old Bluff Highway running parallel to State Highway 1. Follow along on this road, and you'll be protected from traffic by Armco barriers and can rejoin State Highway 1 on the south side of the overbridge.

NEW RIVER ESTUARY TRACK

NORTHERN START	Stead St Wharf
SOUTHERN END	Kekeno Pl
DISTANCE	10.5 km
MAPS	140, 141
TRACK STANDARD	Easy tramping

FOVEAUX WALKWAY

NORTHERN START	Ocean Beach
SOUTHERN END	Stirling Point
DISTANCE	7 km
MAPS	141
TRACK STANDARD	Tramping

JUST BEYOND the old Ocean Beach Freezing Works, a yellow sign points right off State Highway 1 directing you to the start of the Foveaux Walkway. The track leads away uphill through lupins, and heads for the seaward side of Bluff Hill. You're open to the Foveaux Strait weather on this side, and if the westerly is blowing at around its 16 kph average, you'll have a wind-assisted walk. On some days it'll be more supercharged, but whichever, it's a zesty walk.

The track is poled onward through fields of dry grass and rock outcrops. Bluff Hill is a huge pile of norite, but the locals just call it Bluff granite — it's black, it polishes well, and in the small township on the far side of this hill it's the rock they've used on their war memorial.

Foveaux Strait below is shallow, and if the sea is running, you'll see it stirring grey sediments from a sandy bed. Sand oysters love the conditions, and any boat you see is likely to be one of the oyster fleet that works the strait in late summer and autumn.

Three kilometres in, the track leaves the fields to push through flax, then along an increasingly pretty path lined with hebe and native grasses to Lookout Point. From here the track follows the coast, beautifully surfaced, overhung with trees, all its gullies bridged. It's an easy last few kilometres, and if you're a Te Araroa through-tramper this is the end of a journey.

The track emerges onto a tarsealed turning bay. Mainland New Zealand ends here, State Highway 1 ends here, and so does Te Araroa. A yellow AA signpost acknowledges that ending. It bristles with all the distances of the world, but to a Te Araroa tramper, the one that stands out points directly north to Cape Reinga, the lighthouse there, and the start of a long journey. Grip the signpost at Bluff and you've completed a 3000 km tramp end to end of New Zealand.

Through-trampers Eyal Schwartz and Paulus Smit at Lookout Point, Foveaux Walkway.

Trail's end — Bluff signpost.

Glossary

Aggregate	The gravel surface on a road.
Alpine fault	The line through the Southern Alps marking ancient land displacement.
Aotearoa	The Maori name for New Zealand, usually translated as 'land of the long white cloud'.
Aukati	A keep out symbol, or injunction.
Bach	A small usually modest holiday home. Baching is to stay in a bach.
Black smoker	An underwater volcanic vent.
Bluffed	Trapped by an impassable cliff.
Choppered	Moved by helicopter.
Clag	Thick cloud or fog.
Craton	A large block of the earth's crust that has resisted deformation over a geologically long period.
Dacite	A volcanic rock resembling andesite but containing free quartz.
Dune-topper	A house or bach built on a sand dune.
Fault line	The fracture in a rock formation showing land displacement on either side of the fracture.
Fibro	Fibrolite, a fibrous asbestos building material.
Föhn	A warm dry wind on the lee side of a mountain range.
Glaciated	Shaped by a glacier, marked or polished by the action of ice.
Gondwana	The ancient supercontinent, consisting of Antartica, South America, Africa, India, and Australia, and the origin of New Zealand.
Gypsy Day	1 June, when herds of dairy cows are moved to new farms.
Isthmus	A neck of land.
Kaimoana	Food (kai) from the sea (moana).
Kaitiaki	A guardian, trustee. Kaitiakitanga: guardianship, trusteeship.
Kaka	*Nestor meridionalis*. A large dark green forest parrot. Endemic.
Kakariki	*Cyanoramphus novaezelandiae*. A small bright green, red-crowned forest parakeet. Endemic.
Kaumatua	A respected elder or leader.
Kauri	*Agathis australis*. A large straight long-lived tree. Endemic.
Kea	*Nestor notabilis*. A large, bold, dark green mountain parrot. Endemic.
Kereru	*Hemiphaga novaeseelandiae*. New Zealand's large white-fronted bush pigeon. Endemic.
Kiwi	*Apteryx* species. A flightless nocturnal bird, usually a forest dweller.
Koha	A gift or donation of money or food, particularly on a marae, or for services.
Lean-to	A small building attached to a main building.
Loess	Fine wind-blown material from the glacial period.
Long drop	An outside pit toilet.
Mana whenua	The power and authority of the land, or the guardian of that power.
Mana	Power, prestige, honour.
Manuka	*Leptospermum scoparium*. A small-leaved shrub with starlike white or pink flowers. Endemic.
Maori	Normal, ordinary. The native race of Aotearoa.
Massif	A group of mountains.
Matagouri	*Discaria toumatou*. Matakoura. A thick impenetrable spiky alpine shrub Endemic.
Maui	A legendary Maori hero, half-god, half-man, who fished up Aotearoa.
Mere	A fighting club, often carved from pounamu, and held as a treasured heirloom.
Merino huddle	A group of merino sheep tightly bunched together to keep warm.
Moraine	The bank of rocks and rubble left behind by a receding glacier.

Ngati Kuri	A Maori tribe or iwi based in the Far North.
Ngati Wai	A Maori tribe or iwi based along the east coast of Northland.
Norite	A coarse-grained plutonic rock, similar to granite.
Oystercatcher	*Haematopus* species. Torea. Black and white wading bird with a long red bill. Endemic.
Pakeha	Non-Maori New Zealanders, typically of English, Scots and Irish descent.
Papatuanuku	The earth mother in Maori primal legend.
Patu Paraoa	A whalebone club.
Peneplain	A gently undulating, almost featureless plain left by the movement of an ancient river system.
Pied stilt	*Himantopus himantopus*. Poaka. Black and white wading bird with slender pink legs. Native.
Placer gold	Alluvial gold, weathered from the host rock and deposited on a hillside or stream bed.
Plutonic	Rocks formed at great depths in the earth's crust.
Pounamu	New Zealand greenstone.
Pumice	A very light, porous volcanic rock which floats.
Rahui	A ban, usually temporary, to protect seafood, or to prevent trespass.
Roche moutonnée	A rock outcrop shaped by glacial movement, typically with one smooth rounded side.
Rohe	A tribal group, or the territory of that tribal group.
Schist	A coarse-grained metamorphic rock with parallel layers.
Scree	A loose accumulation of sliding broken rock fragments on a hill or mountain side.
Seep	A small spring or moist place where groundwater reaches the earth's surface through an aquifer.
Skid, skid site	A flat area in a forest where logs are prepared for transporting.
Spur	A ridge, an offshoot of the main range.
Standing stock	Keeping cattle or sheep off green feed before transport, to reduce the mess on roads.
Taiaha	A long hardwood weapon with a flat smooth blade.
Tangi	Mourning, the ceremony of mourning after someone has died.
Tarn	A small lake or pool, usually in the mountains.
Te Ika a Maui	The North Island, the fish of Maui.
Te Tau Ihu	The top of the South Island; the grouping of Maori tribes or iwi based there.
Te Wai Pounamu	The South Island, source island for pounamu.
Tectonic plate theory	Geological theory, now accepted, that the earth's crust consists of interlocking plates.
Tern	*Sterna* species. A white and grey bird with sharp red or black bills. Endemic.
The tops	The tops of the hills or mountains — often subject to extreme weather changes.
Top beat	The highest section of hills during a mustering beat.
Tor	An upstanding rocky pile, or peak.
Totara	*Podocarpus totara*. A tall bushy forest tree with small sharp leaves. Endemic.
Tuatua	*Paphies subtriangulata*. A triangle shaped shellfish. Endemic.
Tui	*Prosthemadera novaeseelandiae*. A glossy black songbird with a white throat tuft. Endemic.
Tussock	Alpine snowgrass species, slow-growing. Some species can be 2 m high. Endemic.
Tuwharetoa	A Maori tribe or iwi based in the central North Island.
Urupa	A graveyard or cemetery. Sacred ground.
Waka	A canoe or boat.
Waratah	A metal fence post, used for marking routes in the mountains or high country.
Weekender	A holiday home, likely to be larger than a bach.
Weka	*Gallirallus australis*. A flightless brown bird with a short bill and legs. Very curious. Endemic.
Whanau	The extended family.
Whare runanga	A meeting house.
Wrybill	*Anarhyncus frontalis*. A small grey white wading bird with a bill curved to one side. Endemic.

Image Credits

Acknowledgements (at time of first edition, 2011)

TE ARAROA TRUST

In the beginning, Te Araroa Trust (TAT) was simply the amateur keeper of an idea. It has evolved over the years into a professional unit with the necessary skills to advance the New Zealand-long trail, and to provide specialist legal, mapping, and construction services to Te Araroa's eight regional trusts. TAT chair Roger Wilson has headed this transformation, with excellent negotiation and facilitation skills of his own. The deputy chair, David McGregor, is a senior partner at Bell Gully. His legal experience and knowledge is constantly on call, and he arranged the legal structure of Te Araroa's regional trusts — a critical step in our evolution. Trustee Kim Ollivier of Ollivier and Company undertook the huge task of mapping the trail's constantly evolving line, and now maintains its sophisticated digital mapping and asset management system. Trustee Trevor Butler, managing director of Frame Group Ltd, has brought new standards of planning, building specifications and construction to the trail. Trustee Haunui Royal, Maori Television's general manager, programming, has looked after our marketing.

The late Sir Edmund Hillary was a founding patron of the trust, and opened a number of our tracks. His presence lingers — salutations, Ed. Sir Wilson Whineray is the trust's other founding patron, and remains our patron and advocate.

Te Araroa Trust was formed in 1994. Among those who've served as trustees in the past are David Beattie, Linda Bercusson, John Bould, Michael Fitchett, Warren Gibb, Peter Grayburn, Alison Henry, David Lilly, Neil Macintyre, Fiona Mackenzie, Alison Quesnel, and the late Ray Stroud. We thank them all, and are especially grateful to Jennifer Wheeler and Bob Harvey, former trustees who contributed to the original momentum, and who maintain a strong interest.

Price WaterhouseCoopers have audited our accounts pro bono since the trust's inception — a hugely valuable service. Ken Taylor has served as treasurer and kept the trust's books balanced. Miriam Beatson has been an able secretary since 2002. Noel Sandford, our construction manager, has brought to the trust his outstanding back-country carpentry skills, and his ability to teach every team he leads. The trust's project managers have included Fiona Mackenzie, whose work with councils and landowners amidst the complexities of Northland were critical for the emergence of a viable trail there, and Stefan Seitzer who further developed that trail. More recent project managers include Raewyn Mackenzie who organises the route and the volunteers in the South Auckland region, and Greg Blunden who remains the finisher for the route into Kerikeri. Michael Pullar is TAT's South Island project manager. A long trail walker and runner himself, he scoped many of the memorable routes Te Araroa now uses, and has been tireless in securing them.

THE REGIONAL TRUSTS

Eight regional trusts, the length of New Zealand, have scoped, negotiated, fundraised and arranged construction of their sections of Te Araroa. The trail could not have happened without them. Their voluntary work has been critical to the trail's emergence, they will remain critical to its success ongoing, and they're due a huge round of applause.

In geographical order, the regional trusts are:

Te Araroa Auckland Trust: Raewyn Mackenzie (chair) Sandra Coney, Warren Judd, Ron King, who has been with us, and actively working on route, from the very start, and Norm Sharpe.

Te Araroa Waikato Trust: Margaret Evans (chair), Keith Buswell, Christine Chaplow, Geoffrey Drew, Rt Hon Jim Bolger (patron) and Kevin Were. Past trustees: Graham Haines, Rona Larsen, the late Barry O'Connor, Bill Ward and Marijke Westphal.

Te Araroa Whanganui Trust: Maureen Bamber, Brian Doughty, Ridgway Lythgoe, Annette Main and David Scoullar.

Te Araroa Manawatu Trust: Frank Goldingham (Chair), Gillian Absolon, Heather Bassett, Tony Gates, David Grant, Anthony Lewis and Malcolm Prince. Past trustees: Ian Argyle, Vern Chettleburgh, Christine Cheyne, Brendan Duffy, Jennifer Edwards, Anne Lawrence, Ian McKelvie, Bob Nicholls, Christine Scott, Heather Tanguay, Graham Teahan, and the late John Todd.

Te Araroa Wellington Trust: Bill Wakelin (Chair) Hugh Barr, John Farrell, Ken Fraser, Clelia Lind, Penny Redward, Andrew Simm. Associate trustees: Shelagh Noble, Susanne Pollard and Tricia Walbridge. Past trustees: Robin Chesterfield, the late Denis McLean, who was the founding chair, and Barry Morrison.

Te Araroa Canterbury/West Coast Trust: David Round (chair), John Chapman, Geoff Spearpoint and Marcus Waters.

Te Araroa Otago Trust: Murray Gray, Michael Pullar, Anna Thompson and Gilbert van Reenen.

Te Araroa Southland Trust: Lloyd Blakie (chair), John Fraser, Kevin Hawkes, Robin McNeill and Stuart Tecofsky. Past trustee: the late Warrick McCallum.

VOLUNTEERS AND SUPPORT

Just as TAT serves as a touchstone for the regional trusts, those regional trusts have in turn been the focus of an extended volunteer effort of route finding, funding, construction and maintenance. The community has come in behind the trusts, and the following list of names is extensive, but not exhaustive. It's not possible to note here all the volunteer support or the free or discounted services that have sustained this enterprise from its simple beginnings, and for those many hundreds who've helped and contributed but are not named here, our gratitude also.

Region by region Te Araroa Trust would like to thank:

Northland: Peter Griffiths and Sabrina Raad; Roger Gale; Russell and Cassie Pierce; the Van Beek family; Richard Mecredy; Nigel Cook; Keith and Margaret Day; Mike, Robin and Rowan Taylor; Clayton McInnes; Joyce Palmer; David Edge; Ros and Hugh Cole-Baker; Robert and Kathy Keen; Claudia Edwards and Vivienne Rowell; Jean and Don Goldschmidt; Gunter Haferkamp; Wade and Jan Doak; Te Runanga o Te Rarawa; John McLean and Manukau Maori.

Auckland: Mark and Elaine Percy: Mark has been an outstanding route finder and track maintainer north of Auckland. John Smith — engineer and all round star — has tackled Te Araroa's Te Ara o Puhinui stream in the south of Auckland. Thanks also for sterling work to Chris Morton, Joe Macky, and Judy Begg; Paul Whitfield; Harry Sturme; Chris, Alistair and Richard Todd; Mal Holm; John Gale; Peter Woodhouse; Bruce Ringer; John Hickey; Malcolm Page; Allison Roe; C.K. Stead; Chris Darby; and the Rotary Club of Devonport.

Waikato: Max Harris for critical early work, the students and woodwork teachers from Huntly College, Ngaruawahia High School, St Paul's Collegiate, the Mormon Church College of New Zealand, Te Awamutu College, Hillcrest High School and Hamilton Boys College who built the Pirongia boardwalk sections; RNZAF No.3 Squadron; Te Kuiti Rotary Club; Fonterra Catchment Care programme and New Zealand Conservation Volunteers; Steve Woodward; Tom Roa; Te Ohaaki Marae; Genesis Power Ltd; and Tainui Group Holdings.

Manawatu: Max Batie, Gerry Archey — two great stalwarts; Jarrod Dougherty, Rowan Ellison, and other Bunnings staff; also members of the Manawatu Walkways Promotion Society; Ian Ramson; Dennis Palmer; Penny King; Makahika Outdoor Pursuits Centre; Manawatu 4WD Club; Harvey Jones; Turitea Action Group; Trustpower; NZ Army 2nd Field Engineers; and the Lion Foundation.

Wellington: The late Dr Ian Prior; the Willi Fels Trust; Wellington Rotary Clubs; Kapiti Weekday Walkers; June Rowland; Leon Kiel; Nga Uruora Trust; The Wellington Club; the New Zealand Army; Steve Purchase; and Maria Clement.

Nelson / Marlborough: Pete Brady; Rick Edmonds and all the members of the Link Pathway Group; also Outward Bound staff and students; and Richard Rayner.

Canterbury: Brian Keown and the City Care trainees.

Otago: The Wakatipu Trails Trust; Tim Dennis; John Wellington and all members of the Upper Clutha Tracks Trust; and the former chair, the late John Pawson.

Southland: Brian Keown and City Care trainees; Dr James Ng; the Lions Club.

VOLUNTARY GRANTS OF ACCESS

Landholders who have allowed us across their land when there was no legal necessity for them to do so include: Juken Nissho, *Diggers Valley Road to Waiotehue Road track;* Landcorp's Puketotara Station, and Murray and Julie Wright, *Kerikeri Track;* Sonny George and Karen Herbert from Waikare Marae; Tony Reti and Gary Stowers, *Russell Forest Track;* the Webb brothers, John Robison and Ross Matheson, *Helena Ridge Track;* Don and Val Waetford, Jeff and Betty Carson, and Greta and Craig Harman, *Onekainga Track;* Puketiraki Holdings Ltd, Garth McLeod and Melanie Farr, Nick Davies, Carolyn Taylor and Nicholas Chamberlain, and David Ashby, *Matapouri Bush Track;* Hancock Forest Managers and Peter Houston, *Mackerel Forest Track;* Peter and Sharon Cross, Anne and Alexander Longuet-Higgins, Nickolas and Lynne Sharp, Colin and Alison Christie, and John and Martha Williams, *Te Hikoi o Te Kiri;* Jim Drinnan, Warkworth — permission instead of a paper road; Val and the late Arthur Dunn, *Dunns Track;* Ding Furu of Asia Pacific International (NZ) Ltd, Scott Wilson and Paul Manton, *Puhoi Track;* Landowners between Milford Beach and Takapuna, *Akarana Trail;* Maureen Brophy, donation of land; Mike Peters, Malcolm Entwisle, and Te Ohaaki marae and its elder, Toko Waikato, Maurea marae,

Whatumoana Paki, Mr and Mrs Hill, Pete and Peggy Anderson, A. Fothergill, P.J. and K.A. Watson, D.R. and L.M. Cameron, A. and L. McBride, R.A. and S.A. Kerr, B.J. Laing, Mr and Mrs Scott, the Huntly Golf Club, and R.J. and P.M. Beckett, *Waikato River Track;* Tod Percival, *Mahoe Forest Track.* Kevin and John Were, *Pehitawa Track;* New Zealand Forest Managers and farmers en route, *Mangaokewa River Track;* Hancock Forest Management, *Hauhungaroa Track;* the De Cleene family, *Burttons Track;* Richard Waugh and the Hastings family, *Feilding Route;* Daniel Kilsby, *Mangahao-Makahika Track;* Ontrack / New Zealand Railways Corporation, proposed *Paekakariki Escarpment Track;* John and Mary Carter, *Pukeatua Track;* Kenny and Orla Kyla, and Ewan Wilson, *Daltons Track;* Trustpower, *Arboretum Track;* LINZ, Meridian Energy, transferred 2011 to Genesis Energy, *Tekapo–Twizel Track;* Landcorp, Burwood Station, *Mararoa River Track;* Mutt and Eileen Lange, *Motatapu Alpine Track;* Waterloo Station, Mt Linton Station, *Takitimu Track;* Stephen and Lynda Blair-Eadie, Birchwood Station, and D.T. King and Co, *Woodlaw Track;* Mike and Lorraine Whale, *Island Bush Track;* Graeme Manley, Southland Plantation of NZ Ltd, Waitutu Incorporation, *Longwood Forest Track;* and Oraka-Aparima Runaka, M. Sellars and S. Gillett, P. Westenra and W. Krenz,*Tihaka Beach Track.*

Rayonier Matariki Forests and their forest managers and lawyers deserve special thanks for their consistent help since the mid-1990s: Brian Boyd, Harold Corbett, Sam Middlemass, Peter Spencer and Andy Warren arranged access for Te Araroa through the Waitangi, Mokau, Tutukaka, Waiwhiu, and Kohitere forests in the North Island, and the Woodlaw and Island Bush forests in the South Island.

SPECIAL THANKS

To Margaret Crozier for helping kick it off with our first grant, to Vivian Hutchinson for his faith in us at critical times, to Raewyn White and Derek Tearne of @URL for the web start-up when we couldn't pay much and to Garry Carr for his advice on the geology in this book.

Thanks go to our early walkers — including Eric Martinot and the fabulous Endless Steps Club, who were the first to walk many years ago, and to the dozens since who've come through, ready or not — who have established Te Araroa's credibility, and given practical advice. A significant number of the photographs in this book have come directly from these through and section walkers. TAT also thanks the many individual donors, including some who have made regular monthly payments. They kept us afloat when other funds ran dry.

FUNDERS

Our most substantial private funders have been the ASB Community Trust, the Tindall Foundation, the Mayors Taskforce for Jobs, Trust Waikato, WEL Energy Trust, SkyCity Hamilton, the Perry Foundation, the Gallagher Trust, the New Zealand Lottery Grants Board, the Southern Trust, the Eastern Central Trust, the Community Trust of Southland, and the Stout Trust. We also had help from the Community Employment Group and Taskforce Green subsidies.

COUNCILS

The following councils have supported the trail, with executive staff within them often making special efforts on behalf of Te Araroa. TAT thanks: Northern Regional Council (Marie Slako); Far North District Council (Sue Hodge); Whangarei District Council (Paul McDonald and Glenda Bostwick); Kaipara District Council; the former Rodney District Council (Ian Murray and Peter Galliven); the former North Shore City Council (Damian Herrick and Aimee Mackay); the Auckland Regional Council (principal ranger Tony Oliver and Trudie McNie); the former Manukau City Council (Duncan White and Digby Whyte); Auckland Council (Damien Powley); Waikato District Council; (Allan Turner); Environment Waikato (Warren Stace; Bill McMaster; Terry McDonald and Isy Kennedy); Otorohanga District

Council (Martin Gould); Ruapehu District Council (Warren Furner); Whanganui District Council (Mayor Annette Main and former Mayor Michael Laws); Manawatu District Council; Horowhenua District Council (Mayor Brendan Duffy); Kapiti Coast District Council (Stu Kilmister); Porirua City Council (Mayor Nick Leggett; former Mayor Jenny Brash; Andrew Gray and Jethro Mullen); Wellington City Council (Dave Halliday; former Mayors Mark Blumsky and Kerry Prendergast); Marlborough District Council; Selwyn District Council; Mackenzie District Council; Queenstown Lakes District Council (Paul Wilson); Otago Regional Council (Gerard Collings); Environment Southland (CEO Ciaran Keogh); and Invercargill City Council (Mayor Tim Shadbolt).

WALKING ACCESS COMMISSION

The Walking Access Commission, its regional field advisers and its CEO Mark Neeson have contributed significantly to Te Araroa's success over the past two years, specifically with grants, and through the commission's leadership in opening up walking access.

DEPARTMENT OF CONSERVATION

Since 2007, the most powerful single support for Te Araroa has been the Department of Conservation (DOC). Thanks to the director-general Al Morrison, who championed the Te Araroa funding bid of 2007. The subsequent DOC team assigned to the project was very ably headed by Waikato conservator Greg Martin. His team includes Shaun Sweet, who co-ordinated conservancy effort on public conservation land in the North Island, and Brendon Clough, who drove the South Island programme. This team supervised a very large DOC programme that saw hundreds of kilometres of new Te Araroa trail opened and provided with signage. The DOC staff who have assisted over the past five years are too numerous to mention, but some who have gone out of their way on our behalf include Willie Macrae and Jonathan Maxwell in Northland; Thelma Wilson, Andrew Hill and Matt Ward in Auckland; Bruce Postill and Ray Scrimgeour in Waikato; Wayne Boness and Ian Cooksley in Wellington; Mark Nelson and Alison Rothschild in Nelson/Tasman; Murray Thomas, Ronan Grew, Chris Stewart, and Ian Guthrie in Canterbury; Jeff Connell and Paul Hellebrekers in Otago; and Dave Taylor, Brian Murphy, Ken Bradley, Keri Tuna and Philippa Christie in Southland.

Three successive prime ministers gave Te Araroa profile and credibility. Jim Bolger opened the first track at Waitangi in 1995. Helen Clark was a great supporter who liked to open new linking trails — and walk them — on her birthday. She helped Te Araroa score its first significant government funding in 2007. David Parker, former Minister for Land Information, guided our South Island routes into the final Crown Tenure Review settlements. John Key opened the high-profile track across the Pirongia summit in 2009, and surprised the trust in 2011, a year which saw huge callouts of government money, with a 'fiscally neutral' transfer of funding out of the cycleways budget to help build Te Araroa's last walking track links.

Thanks to Roger Smith and his team at Geographx for their excellent maps, and to Nicola Legat, Rebecca Lal and the team at Random House for their hard and detailed work against deadline.

Finally my thanks to my wife and family for their support through the last 15 years.

Geoff Chapple
Founder, Te Araroa Trust
2011